# scikit-learn Cookbook

Over 50 recipes to incorporate scikit-learn into every step
of the data science pipeline, from feature extraction to
model building and model evaluation

**Trent Hauck**

[PACKT] open source*
PUBLISHING     community experience distilled

BIRMINGHAM - MUMBAI

# scikit-learn Cookbook

Copyright © 2014 Packt Publishing

First published: November 2014

Production reference: 1271014

Published by Packt Publishing Ltd.
Livery Place
35 Livery Street
Birmingham B3 2PB, UK.

ISBN 978-1-78398-948-5

www.packtpub.com

# Credits

**Author**

Trent Hauck

**Reviewers**

Anoop Thomas Mathew

Xingzhong

**Commissioning Editor**

Kunal Parikh

**Acquisition Editor**

Owen Roberts

**Content Development Editor**

Dayan Hyames

**Technical Editors**

Mrunal M. Chavan

Dennis John

**Copy Editors**

Janbal Dharmaraj

Sayanee Mukherjee

**Project Coordinator**

Harshal Ved

**Proofreaders**

Simran Bhogal

Bridget Braund

Amy Johnson

**Indexer**

Tejal Soni

**Graphics**

Sheetal Aute

Ronak Dhruv

Abhinash Sahu

**Production Coordinator**

Manu Joseph

**Cover Work**

Manu Joseph

# About the Author

**Trent Hauck** is a data scientist living and working in the Seattle area. He grew up in Wichita, Kansas and received his undergraduate and graduate degrees from the University of Kansas.

He is the author of the book *Instant Data Intensive Apps with pandas How-to*, *Packt Publishing*—a book that can get you up to speed quickly with pandas and other associated technologies.

First, a big thanks to the Python software community, the people behind scikit-learn in particular; the skill with which the code is developed is responsible for a lot of good work that gets done.

Personally, I'd like to thank my family, friends, and coworkers.

# About the Reviewers

**Anoop Thomas Mathew** is a software architect with years of experience in working with Python and software development in general. With the title of Chief Technology Officer at Profoundis Inc., he leads the engineering efforts at Profoundis and is now focusing on `https://vibeapp.co`. He has spoken at conferences such as The Fifth Elephant 2012, PyCon 2012, FOSSMeet 2013, PyCon 2013, and FOSSMeet 2014 to name a few. He blogs at `http://infiniteloop.in`.

He is the author of the book, *Code Explorer's Guide to the Open Source Jungle*, available online at `https://leanpub.com/opensourcebook`.

---

To my beloved.

---

**Xingzhong** is a PhD candidate in Electrical Engineering at Stevens Institute of Technology, Hoboken, New Jersey, where he works as a research assistant, designing and implementing machine-learning models in computer vision and signal processing applications.

Although Python is his primary programming language, occasionally, for fun and curiosity, his works might be written on golang, Scala, JavaScript, and so on. As a self-confessed technology geek, he is passionate about exploring new software and hardware.

# www.PacktPub.com

## Support files, eBooks, discount offers, and more

For support files and downloads related to your book, please visit www.PacktPub.com.

Did you know that Packt offers eBook versions of every book published, with PDF and ePub files available? You can upgrade to the eBook version at www.PacktPub.com and as a print book customer, you are entitled to a discount on the eBook copy. Get in touch with us at service@packtpub.com for more details.

At www.PacktPub.com, you can also read a collection of free technical articles, sign up for a range of free newsletters and receive exclusive discounts and offers on Packt books and eBooks.

http://PacktLib.PacktPub.com

Do you need instant solutions to your IT questions? PacktLib is Packt's online digital book library. Here, you can search, access, and read Packt's entire library of books.

## Why subscribe?

- ▸ Fully searchable across every book published by Packt
- ▸ Copy and paste, print, and bookmark content
- ▸ On demand and accessible via a web browser

## Free access for Packt account holders

If you have an account with Packt at www.PacktPub.com, you can use this to access PacktLib today and view 9 entirely free books. Simply use your login credentials for immediate access.

# Table of Contents

# Preface

This book is designed in the same way that many data science and analytics projects play out. First, we need to acquire data; the data is often messy, incomplete, or not correct in some way. Therefore, we spend the first chapter talking about strategies for dealing with bad data and ways to deal with other problems that arise from data. For example, what happens if we have too many features? How do we handle that? The first chapter is your guide. The meat of the book will walk you through various algorithms and how to implement them into your workflow. And finally, we'll end with the postmodel workflow. This chapter is fairly agnostic to the other chapters and can be applied to the various algorithms you'll learn up until the final chapter.

## What this book covers

*Chapter 1, Premodel Workflow*, walks you through the preparatory step of preparing a dataset for modeling and shows how scikit-learn can help to ameliorate the burden of preprocessing.

*Chapter 2, Working with Linear Models*, discusses how many problems can be viewed as linear models upon the appropriate application of a transformation, and therefore walks you through what may be the most used class of models.

*Chapter 3, Building Models with Distance Metrics*, encompasses a large number of topics that largely work by measuring the similarity between the data points. Because similarity and distance are often synonymous, clustering can often be used as long as a distance function can be defined.

*Chapter 4, Classifying Data with scikit-learn*, focuses on the various methods within scikit-learn that are used to determine a data point as some member between 1 and N classes.

*Chapter 5, Postmodel Workflow*, teaches us how we can take a basic model produced from one of the recipes and tune it so that we can achieve better results than we could with the basic model.

# What you need for this book

Here are the contents of the `requirements.txt` file that will get the environment set up. This will allow you to follow along with the code in the book.

I've also included a conda requirements file; this method may be easier for less-experienced Python developers:

```
dateutil==2.1
ipython==2.2.0
ipython-notebook==2.1.0
jinja2==2.7.3
markupsafe==0.18
matplotlib==1.3.1
numpy==1.8.1
patsy==0.3.0
pandas==0.14.1
pip==1.5.6
pydot==1.0.28
pyparsing==1.5.6
pytz==2014.4
pyzmq==14.3.1
scikit-learn==0.15.0
scipy==0.14.0
setuptools==3.6
six==1.7.3
ssl_match_hostname==3.4.0.2
tornado==3.2.2
```

# Who this book is for

This book can help budding analysts who are familiar with Python to take the next step into machine learning with scikit-learn. It is assumed that you are familiar with Python, but beyond that we'll touch on many of the important aspects of scikit-learn. On top of that, we'll discuss enough theory to help you ask the next question after you've figured out the nuances of scikit-learn.

# Sections

This book contains the following sections:

## Getting ready

This section tells us what to expect in the recipe, and describes how to set up any software or any preliminary settings needed for the recipe.

# How to do it...

This section characterizes the steps to be followed for "cooking" the recipe.

# How it works...

This section usually consists of a brief and detailed explanation of what happened in the previous section.

# There's more...

This consists of additional information about the recipe in order to make the reader more anxious about the recipe.

# See also

This section may contain references to the recipe.

# Conventions

In this book, you will find a number of styles of text that distinguish between different kinds of information. Here are some examples of these styles, and an explanation of their meaning.

Code words in text, database table names, folder names, filenames, file extensions, pathnames, dummy URLs, user input, and Twitter handles are shown as follows: "From within IPython, run `datasets.*?`, which will list everything available within the `datasets` module."

Any command-line input or output is written as follows:

```
>>> transformed = dl.fit_transform(iris_data[::2])
>>> transformed[:5]
```

**New terms** and **important words** are shown in bold. Words that you see on the screen, in menus or dialog boxes for example, appear in the text like this: "Notice the peak around **0**. This will naturally lead to the zero coefficients in lasso regression."

Warnings or important notes appear in a box like this.

Tips and tricks appear like this.

# Reader feedback

Feedback from our readers is always welcome. Let us know what you think about this book—what you liked or may have disliked. Reader feedback is important for us to develop titles that you really get the most out of.

To send us general feedback, simply send an e-mail to feedback@packtpub.com, and mention the book title via the subject of your message.

If there is a topic that you have expertise in and you are interested in either writing or contributing to a book, see our author guide on www.packtpub.com/authors.

# Customer support

Now that you are the proud owner of a Packt book, we have a number of things to help you to get the most from your purchase.

## Downloading the example code

You can download the example code files for all Packt books you have purchased from your account at http://www.packtpub.com. If you purchased this book elsewhere, you can visit http://www.packtpub.com/support and register to have the files e-mailed directly to you.

## Downloading the color images of this book

We also provide you a PDF file that has color images of the screenshots/diagrams used in this book. The color images will help you better understand the changes in the output. You can download this file from: https://www.packtpub.com/sites/default/files/downloads/9485OS_GraphicsBundle.pdf.

## Errata

Although we have taken every care to ensure the accuracy of our content, mistakes do happen. If you find a mistake in one of our books—maybe a mistake in the text or the code—we would be grateful if you would report this to us. By doing so, you can save other readers from frustration and help us improve subsequent versions of this book. If you find any errata, please report them by visiting http://www.packtpub.com/submit-errata, selecting your book, clicking on the **errata submission form** link, and entering the details of your errata. Once your errata are verified, your submission will be accepted and the errata will be uploaded on our website, or added to any list of existing errata, under the Errata section of that title. Any existing errata can be viewed by selecting your title from http://www.packtpub.com/support.

# Piracy

Piracy of copyright material on the Internet is an ongoing problem across all media. At Packt, we take the protection of our copyright and licenses very seriously. If you come across any illegal copies of our works, in any form, on the Internet, please provide us with the location address or website name immediately so that we can pursue a remedy.

Please contact us at copyright@packtpub.com with a link to the suspected pirated material.

We appreciate your help in protecting our authors, and our ability to bring you valuable content.

# Questions

You can contact us at questions@packtpub.com if you are having a problem with any aspect of the book, and we will do our best to address it.

# 1

# Premodel Workflow

This chapter will cover the following topics:

- ▸ Getting sample data from external sources
- ▸ Creating sample data for toy analysis
- ▸ Confirming the characteristics of created data
- ▸ Scaling data to the standard normal
- ▸ Creating binary features through thresholding
- ▸ Working with categorical variables
- ▸ Binarizing label features
- ▸ Imputing missing values through various strategies
- ▸ Using Pipelines for multiple preprocessing steps
- ▸ Reducing dimensionality with PCA
- ▸ Using factor analytics for decomposition
- ▸ Kernel PCA for nonlinear dimensionality reduction
- ▸ Using truncated SVD to reduce dimensionality
- ▸ Decomposition to classify with DictionaryLearning
- ▸ Putting it all together with Pipelines
- ▸ Using Gaussian processes for regression
- ▸ Defining the Gaussian process object directly
- ▸ Using stochastic gradient descent for regression

# Introduction

This chapter discusses setting data, preparing data, and premodel dimensionality reduction. These are not the attractive parts of **machine learning (ML)**, but they often turn out to be what determines if a model will work or not.

There are three main parts to the chapter. Firstly, we'll create fake data; this might seem trivial, but creating fake data and fitting models to fake data is an important step in model testing. It's more useful in situations where we implement an algorithm from scratch, but I'll cover it here for completeness, and in the event you don't have data of your own, you can just create it. Secondly, we'll look at broadly handling data transformations as a preprocessing step, which includes data imputation, categorical variable encoding, and so on. Thirdly, we'll look at situations where we have a large number of features relative to the number of observations we have.

This chapter, especially the first half, will set the stage for the later chapters. In order to use scikit-learn, data is required. The first two sections will discuss acquiring the data; the rest of the first half will discuss preparing this data for use.

This book is written using scikit-learn 0.15, NumPy 1.9, and pandas 0.13. There are other packages used as well, so it's advisable that you refer to the installation instructions included in this book.

# Getting sample data from external sources

If possible, try working with a familiar dataset while working through this book; in order to level the field, built-in datasets will be used. The built-in datasets can be used as stand-ins to test several different modeling techniques such as regression and classification. These are, for the most part, famous datasets. This is very useful as papers in various fields will often use these datasets for authors to put forth how their model fits as compared to other models.

I recommend you use IPython to run these commands as they are presented. Muscle memory is important, and it's best to get to the point where basic commands take no extra mental effort. An even better way might be to run IPython Notebook. If you do, make sure to use the `%matplotlib inline` command; this will allow you to see the plots in Notebook.

## Getting ready

The datasets in scikit-learn are contained within the `datasets` module. Use the following command to import these datasets:

```
>>> from sklearn import datasets
>>> import numpy as np
```

From within IPython, run `datasets.*?`, which will list everything available within the `datasets` module.

## How to do it...

There are two main types of data within the `datasets` module. Smaller test datasets are included in the `sklearn` package and can be viewed by running `datasets.load_*?`. Larger datasets are also available for download as required. The latter are not included in `sklearn` by default; however, at times, they are better to test models and algorithms due to sufficient complexity to represent realistic situations.

Datasets are included with `sklearn` by default; to view these datasets, run `datasets.load_*?`. There are other types of datasets that must be fetched. These datasets are larger, and therefore, they do not come within the package. This said, they are often better to test algorithms that might be used in the wild.

First, load the `boston` dataset and examine it:

```
>>> boston = datasets.load_boston()
>>> print boston.DESCR #output omitted due to length
```

`DESCR` will present a basic overview of the data to give you some context.

Next, fetch a dataset:

```
>>> housing = datasets.fetch_california_housing()
downloading Cal. housing from http://lib.stat.cmu.edu [...]

>>> print housing.DESCR #output omitted due to length
```

## How it works...

When these datasets are loaded, they aren't loaded as NumPy arrays. They are of type `Bunch`. A **Bunch** is a common data structure in Python. It's essentially a dictionary with the keys added to the object as attributes.

To access the data using the (surprise!) `data` attribute, which is a NumPy array containing the independent variables, the target attribute has the dependent variable:

```
>>> X, y = boston.data, boston.target
```

There are various implementations available on the Web for the `Bunch` object; it's not too difficult to write on your own. scikit-learn defines `Bunch` (as of this writing) in the base module.

It's available in GitHub at `https://github.com/scikit-learn/scikit-learn/blob/master/sklearn/datasets/base.py`.

## There's more...

When you fetch a dataset from an external source it will, by default, place the data in your home directory under `scikit_learn_data/`; this behavior is configurable in two ways:

   ▶   To modify the default behavior, set the `SCIKIT_LEARN_DATA` environment variable to point to the desired folder.
   ▶   The first argument of the fetch methods is `data_home`, which will specify the home folder on a case-by-case basis.

It is easy to check the default location by calling `datasets.get_data_home()`.

## See also

The **UCI Machine Learning Repository** is a great place to find sample datasets. Many of the datasets in scikit-learn are hosted here; however, there are more datasets available. Other notable sources include KDD, your local government agency, and Kaggle competitions.

# Creating sample data for toy analysis

I will again implore you to use some of your own data for this book, but in the event you cannot, we'll learn how we can use scikit-learn to create toy data.

## Getting ready

Very similar to getting built-in datasets, fetching new datasets, and creating sample datasets, the functions that are used follow the naming convention `make_<the data set>`. Just to be clear, this data is purely artificial:

```
>>> datasets.make_*?
datasets.make_biclusters
datasets.make_blobs
```

```
datasets.make_checkerboard
datasets.make_circles
datasets.make_classification
...
```

To save typing, import the `datasets` module as `d` , and `numpy` as `np`:

```
>>> import sklearn.datasets as d
>>> import numpy as np
```

## How to do it...

This section will walk you through the creation of several datasets; the following *How it works...* section will confirm the purported characteristics of the datasets. In addition to the sample datasets, these will be used throughout the book to create data with the necessary characteristics for the algorithms on display.

First, the stalwart—regression:

```
>>> reg_data = d.make_regression()
```

By default, this will generate a tuple with a 100 x 100 matrix – 100 samples by 100 features. However, by default, only 10 features are responsible for the target data generation. The second member of the tuple is the target variable.

It is also possible to get more involved. For example, to generate a 1000 x 10 matrix with five features responsible for the target creation, an underlying bias factor of 1.0, and 2 targets, the following command will be run:

```
>>> complex_reg_data = d.make_regression(1000, 10, 5, 2, 1.0)
>>> complex_reg_data[0].shape
(1000, 10)
```

Classification datasets are also very simple to create. It's simple to create a base classification set, but the basic case is rarely experienced in practice—most users don't convert, most transactions aren't fraudulent, and so on. Therefore, it's useful to explore classification on unbalanced datasets:

```
>>> classification_set = d.make_classification(weights=[0.1])
>>> np.bincount(classification_set[1])
array([10, 90])
```

Clusters will also be covered. There are actually several functions to create datasets that can be modeled by different cluster algorithms. For example, `blobs` are very easy to create and can be modeled by K-Means:

```
>>> blobs = d.make_blobs()
```

This will look like the following:

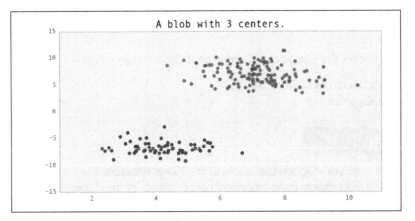

## How it works...

Let's walk you through how scikit-learn produces the regression dataset by taking a look at the source code (with some modifications for clarity). Any undefined variables are assumed to have the default value of `make_regression`.

It's actually surprisingly simple to follow.

First, a random array is generated with the size specified when the function is called:

```
>>> X = np.random.randn(n_samples, n_features)
```

Given the basic dataset, the target dataset is then generated:

```
>>> ground_truth = np.zeroes((np_samples, n_target))
>>> ground_truth[:n_informative, :] = 100*np.random.rand(n_informative,
    n_targets)
```

The dot product of X and `ground_truth` are taken to get the final target values. Bias, if any, is added at this time:

```
>>> y = np.dot(X, ground_truth) + bias
```

 The dot product is simply a matrix multiplication. So, our final dataset will have `n_samples`, which is the number of rows from the dataset, and `n_target`, which is the number of target variables.

Due to NumPy's broadcasting, bias can be a scalar value, and this value will be added to every sample.

Finally, it's a simple matter of adding any noise and shuffling the dataset. Voilà, we have a dataset perfect to test regression.

# Scaling data to the standard normal

A preprocessing step that is almost recommended is to scale columns to the standard normal. The **standard normal** is probably the most important distribution of all statistics.

If you've ever been introduced to statistics, you must have almost certainly seen **z-scores**. In truth, that's all this recipe is about—transforming our features from their endowed distribution into z-scores.

## Getting ready

The act of scaling data is extremely useful. There are a lot of machine learning algorithms, which perform differently (and incorrectly) in the event the features exist at different scales. For example, SVMs perform poorly if the data isn't scaled because it uses a distance function in its optimization, which is biased if one feature varies from 0 to 10,000 and the other varies from 0 to 1.

The `preprocessing` module contains several useful functions to scale features:

```
>>> from sklearn import preprocessing
>>> import numpy as np # we'll need it later
```

## How to do it...

Continuing with the `boston` dataset, run the following commands:

```
>>> X[:, :3].mean(axis=0) #mean of the first 3 features
array([  3.59376071,  11.36363636,  11.13677866])
>>> X[:, :3].std(axis=0)
array([  8.58828355,  23.29939569,   6.85357058])
```

There's actually a lot to learn from this initially. Firstly, the first feature has the smallest mean but varies even more than the third feature. The second feature has the largest mean and standard deviation—it takes the widest spread of values:

```
>>> X_2 = preprocessing.scale(X[:, :3])

>>> X_2.mean(axis=0)
array([  6.34099712e-17,  -6.34319123e-16,  -2.68291099e-15])

>>> X_2.std(axis=0)
array([ 1.,  1.,  1.])
```

## How it works...

The center and scaling function is extremely simple. It merely subtracts the mean and divides by the standard deviation:

$$x = \frac{x - \overline{x}}{\sigma}$$

In addition to a function, there is also a center and scaling class that is easy to invoke, and this is particularly useful when used in conjunction with the Pipelines mentioned later. It's also useful for the center and scaling class to persist across individual scaling:

```
>>> my_scaler = preprocessing.StandardScaler()
>>> my_scaler.fit(X[:, :3])
>>> my_scaler.transform(X[:, :3]).mean(axis=0)
array([  6.34099712e-17,  -6.34319123e-16,  -2.68291099e-15])
```

Scaling features to mean 0, and standard deviation 1 isn't the only useful type of scaling. Preprocessing also contains a `MinMaxScaler` class, which will scale the data within a certain range:

```
>>> my_minmax_scaler = preprocessing.MinMaxScaler()
>>> my_minmax_scaler.fit(X[:, :3])
>>> my_minmax_scaler.transform(X[:, :3]).max(axis=0)
array([ 1.,   1.,   1.])
```

It's very simple to change the minimum and maximum values of the `MinMaxScaler` class from its default of 0 and 1, respectively:

```
>>> my_odd_scaler = preprocessing.MinMaxScaler(feature_range=(-3.14,
                                                               3.14))
```

Furthermore, another option is **normalization**. This will scale each sample to have a length of 1. This is different from the other types of scaling done previously, where the features were scaled. Normalization is illustrated in the following command:

```
>>> normalized_X = preprocessing.normalize(X[:, :3])
```

If it's not apparent why this is useful, consider the Euclidian distance (a measure of similarity) between three of the samples, where one sample has the values (1, 1, 0), another has (3, 3, 0), and the final has (1, -1, 0).

The distance between the 1ˢᵗ and 3ʳᵈ vector is less than the distance between the 1ˢᵗ and 2ⁿᵈ though the 1ˢᵗ and 3ʳᵈ are orthogonal, whereas the 1ˢᵗ and 2ⁿᵈ only differ by a scalar factor of 3. Since distances are often used as measures of similarity, not normalizing the data first will be misleading..

## There's more...

Imputation is a very deep subject. Here are a few things to consider when using scikit-learn's implementation.

### Creating idempotent scalar objects

It is possible to scale the mean and/or variance in the `StandardScaler` instance. For instance, it's possible (though not useful) to create a `StandardScaler` instance, which simply performs the identity transformation:

```
>>> my_useless_scaler = preprocessing.StandardScaler(with_mean=False,
                                                     with_std=False)
>>> transformed_sd = my_useless_scaler
                    .fit_transform(X[:, :3]).std(axis=0)
>>> original_sd = X[:, :3].std(axis=0)
>>> np.array_equal(transformed_sd, original_sd)
```

### Handling sparse imputations

Sparse matrices aren't handled differently from normal matrices when doing scaling. This is because to mean center the data, the data will have its 0s altered to nonzero values, thus the matrix will no longer be sparse:

```
>>> matrix = scipy.sparse.eye(1000)
>>> preprocessing.scale(matrix)
...
ValueError: Cannot center sparse matrices: pass 'with_mean=False' instead
See docstring for motivation and alternatives.
```

As noted in the error, it is possible to scale a sparse matrix `with_std` only:

```
>>> preprocessing.scale(matrix, with_mean=False)
<1000x1000 sparse matrix of type '<type 'numpy.float64'>'
        with 1000 stored elements in Compressed Sparse Row format>
```

The other option is to call `todense()` on the array. However, this is dangerous because the matrix is already sparse for a reason, and it will potentially cause a memory error.

# Creating binary features through thresholding

In the last recipe, we looked at transforming our data into the standard normal distribution. Now, we'll talk about another transformation, one that is quite different.

Instead of working with the distribution to standardize it, we'll purposely throw away data; but, if we have good reason, this can be a very smart move. Often, in what is ostensibly continuous data, there are discontinuities that can be determined via binary features.

## Getting ready

Creating binary features and outcomes is a very useful method, but it should be used with caution. Let's use the `boston` dataset to learn how to create turn values in binary outcomes.

First, load the `boston` dataset:

```
>>> from sklearn import datasets
>>> boston = datasets.load_boston()
>>> import numpy as np
```

## How to do it...

Similar to scaling, there are two ways to binarize features in scikit-learn:

- `preprocessing.binarize #(a function)`
- `preprocessing.Binarizer #(a class)`

The `boston` dataset's target variable is the median value of houses in thousands. This dataset is good to test regression and other continuous predictors, but consider a situation where we want to simply predict if a house's value is more than the overall mean. To do this, we will want to create a threshold value of the mean. If the value is greater than the mean, produce a 1; if it is less, produce a 0:

```
>>> from sklearn import preprocessing
>>> new_target = preprocessing.binarize(boston.target,
                    threshold=boston.target.mean())
>>> new_target[:5]
array([ 1.,  0.,  1.,  1.,  1.])
```

This was easy, but let's check to make sure it worked correctly:

```
>>> (boston.target[:5] > boston.target.mean()).astype(int)
array([1, 0, 1, 1, 1])
```

Given the simplicity of the operation in NumPy, it's a fair question to ask why you will want to use the built-in functionality of scikit-learn. Pipelines, covered in the *Using Pipelines for multiple preprocessing steps* recipe, will go far to explain this; in anticipation of this, let's use the `Binarizer` class:

```
>>> bin = preprocessing.Binarizer(boston.target.mean())
>>> new_target = bin.fit_transform(boston.target)
>>> new_target[:5]
array([ 1.,   0.,   1.,   1.,   1.])
```

## How it works...

Hopefully, this is pretty obvious; but under the hood, scikit-learn creates a conditional mask that is `True` if the value in the array in question is more than the threshold. It then updates the array to 1 where the condition is met, and 0 where it is not.

## There's more...

Let's also learn about sparse matrices and the `fit` method.

### Sparse matrices

Sparse matrices are special in that zeros aren't stored; this is done in an effort to save space in memory. This creates an issue for the binarizer, so to combat it, a special condition for the binarizer for sparse matrices is that the threshold cannot be less than zero:

```
>>> from scipy.sparse import coo
>>> spar = coo.coo_matrix(np.random.binomial(1, .25, 100))
>>> preprocessing.binarize(spar, threshold=-1)
ValueError: Cannot binarize a sparse matrix with threshold < 0
```

### The fit method

The `fit` method exists for the binarizer transformation, but it will not fit anything, it will simply return the object.

## Working with categorical variables

Categorical variables are a problem. On one hand they provide valuable information; on the other hand, it's probably text—either the actual text or integers corresponding to the text—like an index in a lookup table.

So, we clearly need to represent our text as integers for the model's sake, but we can't just use the `id` field or naively represent them. This is because we need to avoid a similar problem to the *Creating binary features through thresholding* recipe. If we treat data that is continuous, it must be interpreted as continuous.

## Getting ready

The `boston` dataset won't be useful for this section. While it's useful for feature binarization, it won't suffice for creating features from categorical variables. For this, the `iris` dataset will suffice.

For this to work, the problem needs to be turned on its head. Imagine a problem where the goal is to predict the sepal width; therefore, the species of the flower will probably be useful as a feature.

Let's get the data sorted first:

```
>>> from sklearn import datasets
>>> iris = datasets.load_iris()
>>> X = iris.data
>>> y = iris.target
```

Now, with X and Y being as they normally will be, we'll operate on the data as one:

```
>>> import numpy as np
>>> d = np.column_stack((X, y))
```

## How to do it...

Convert the text columns to three features:

```
>>> from sklearn import preprocessing
>>> text_encoder = preprocessing.OneHotEncoder()
>>> text_encoder.fit_transform(d[:, -1:]).toarray()[:5]
array([[ 1.,   0.,   0.],
       [ 1.,   0.,   0.],
       [ 1.,   0.,   0.],
       [ 1.,   0.,   0.],
       [ 1.,   0.,   0.]])
```

## How it works...

The encoder creates additional features for each categorical variable, and the value returned is a sparse matrix. The result is a sparse matrix by definition; each row of the new features has 0 everywhere, except for the column whose value is associated with the feature's category. Therefore, it makes sense to store this data in a sparse matrix.

`text_encoder` is now a standard scikit-learn model, which means that it can be used again:

```
>>> text_encoder.transform(np.ones((3, 1))).toarray()
array([[ 0.,   1.,   0.],
       [ 0.,   1.,   0.],
       [ 0.,   1.,   0.]])
```

## There's more...

Other options exist to create categorical variables in scikit-learn and Python at large. `DictVectorizer` is a good option if you like to limit the dependencies of your projects to only scikit-learn and you have a fairly simple encoding scheme. However, if you require more sophisticated categorical encoding, `patsy` is a very good option.

### DictVectorizer

Another option is to use `DictVectorizer`. This can be used to directly convert strings to features:

```
>>> from sklearn.feature_extraction import DictVectorizer
>>> dv = DictVectorizer()
>>> my_dict = [{'species': iris.target_names[i]} for i in y]
>>> dv.fit_transform(my_dict).toarray()[:5]
array([[ 1.,    0.,    0.],
       [ 1.,    0.,    0.],
       [ 1.,    0.,    0.],
       [ 1.,    0.,    0.],
       [ 1.,    0.,    0.]])
```

 Dictionaries can be viewed as a sparse matrix. They only contain entries for the nonzero values.

### Patsy

`patsy` is another package useful to encode categorical variables. Often used in conjunction with `StatsModels`, `patsy` can turn an array of strings into a design matrix.

This section does not directly pertain to scikit-learn; therefore, skipping it is okay without impacting the understanding of how scikit-learn works.

For example, `dm = patsy.design_matrix("x + y")` will create the appropriate columns if x or y are strings. If they aren't, `C(x)` inside the formula will signify that it is a categorical variable.

For example, `iris.target` can be interpreted as a continuous variable if we don't know better. Therefore, use the following command:

```
>>> import patsy
>>> patsy.dmatrix("0 + C(species)", {'species': iris.target})
DesignMatrix with shape (150, 3)
```

| C(species)[0] | C(species)[1] | C(species)[2] |
|:---:|:---:|:---:|
| 1 | 0 | 0 |
| 1 | 0 | 0 |
| 1 | 0 | 0 |
| 1 | 0 | 0 |
| 1 | 0 | 0 |
| 1 | 0 | 0 |
| 1 | 0 | 0 |
| 1 | 0 | 0 |
| 1 | 0 | 0 |

[...]

# Binarizing label features

In this recipe, we'll look at working with categorical variables in a different way. In the event that only one or two categories of the feature are important, it might be wise to avoid the extra dimensionality, which might be created if there are several categories.

## Getting ready

There's another way to work with categorical variables. Instead of dealing with the categorical variables using `OneHotEncoder`, we can use `LabelBinarizer`. This is a combination of thresholding and working with categorical variables.

To show how this works, load the `iris` dataset:

```
>>> from sklearn import datasets as d
>>> iris = d.load_iris()
>>> target = iris.target
```

## How to do it...

Import the `LabelBinarizer()` method and create an object:

```
>>> from sklearn.preprocessing import LabelBinarizer
>>> label_binarizer = LabelBinarizer()
```

Now, simply transform the target outcomes to the new feature space:

```
>>> new_target = label_binarizer.fit_transform(target)
```

Let's look at `new_target` and the `label_binarizer` object to get a feel of what happened:

```
>>> new_target.shape
(150, 3)
```

```
>>> new_target[:5]
array([[1, 0, 0],
       [1, 0, 0],
       [1, 0, 0],
       [1, 0, 0],
       [1, 0, 0]])

>>> new_target[-5:]
array([[0, 0, 1],
       [0, 0, 1],
       [0, 0, 1],
       [0, 0, 1],
       [0, 0, 1]])

>>> label_binarizer.classes_
array([0, 1, 2])
```

## How it works...

The `iris` target has a cardinality of 3, that is, it has three unique values. When `LabelBinarizer` converts the vector *N x 1* into the vector *N x C*, where *C* is the cardinality of the *N x 1* dataset, it is important to note that once the object has been fit, introducing unseen values in the transformation will throw an error:

```
>>> label_binarizer.transform([4])
[...]
ValueError: classes [0 1 2] mismatch with the labels [4] found in the
data
```

## There's more...

Zero and one do not have to represent the positive and negative instances of the target value. For example, if we want positive values to be represented by 1,000, and negative values to be represented by -1,000, we'd simply make the designation when we create `label_binarizer`:

```
>>> label_binarizer = LabelBinarizer(neg_label=-1000, pos_label=1000)
>>> label_binarizer.fit_transform(target)[:5]
array([[ 1000, -1000, -1000],
       [ 1000, -1000, -1000],
       [ 1000, -1000, -1000],
       [ 1000, -1000, -1000],
       [ 1000, -1000, -1000]])
```

> The only restriction on the positive and negative values is that they must be integers.

# Imputing missing values through various strategies

Data imputation is critical in practice, and thankfully there are many ways to deal with it. In this recipe, we'll look at a few of the strategies. However, be aware that there might be other approaches that fit your situation better.

This means scikit-learn comes with the ability to perform fairly common imputations; it will simply apply some transformations to the existing data and fill the NAs. However, if the dataset is missing data, and there's a known reason for this missing data—for example, response times for a server that times out after 100ms—it might be better to take a statistical approach through other packages such as the Bayesian treatment via PyMC, the Hazard Models via Lifelines, or something home-grown.

## Getting ready

The first thing to do to learn how to input missing values is to create missing values. NumPy's masking will make this extremely simple:

```
>>> from sklearn import datasets
>>> import numpy as np
>>> iris = datasets.load_iris()
>>> iris_X = iris.data
>>> masking_array = np.random.binomial(1, .25,
                        iris_X.shape).astype(bool)
>>> iris_X[masking_array] = np.nan
```

To unravel this a bit, in case NumPy isn't too familiar, it's possible to index arrays with other arrays in NumPy. So, to create the random missing data, a random Boolean array is created, which is of the same shape as the `iris` dataset. Then, it's possible to make an assignment via the masked array. It's important to note that because a random array is used, it is likely your `masking_array` will be different from what's used here.

To make sure this works, use the following command (since we're using a random mask, it might not match directly):

```
>>> masking_array[:5]
array([[False, False, False, False],
       [False, False, False, False],
       [False, False, False, False],
       [ True, False, False, False],
       [False, False, False, False]], dtype=bool)
>>> iris_X [:5]
array([[ 5.1,  3.5,  1.4,  0.2],
       [ 4.9,  3. ,  1.4,  0.2],
```

```
    [ 4.7,   3.2,   1.3,   0.2],
    [ nan,   3.1,   1.5,   0.2],
    [ 5. ,   3.6,   1.4,   0.2]])
```

## How to do it...

A theme prevalent throughout this book (due to the theme throughout scikit-learn) is reusable classes that fit and transform datasets and that can subsequently be used to transform unseen datasets. This is illustrated as follows:

```
>>> from sklearn import preprocessing
>>> impute = preprocessing.Imputer()
>>> iris_X_prime = impute.fit_transform(iris_X)
>>> iris_X_prime[:5]
array([[ 5.1        ,  3.5       ,  1.4       ,  0.2       ],
       [ 4.9        ,  3.       ,  1.4       ,  0.2       ],
       [ 4.7        ,  3.2       ,  1.3       ,  0.2       ],
       [ 5.87923077,  3.1       ,  1.5       ,  0.2       ],
       [ 5.        ,  3.6       ,  1.4       ,  0.2       ]])
```

Notice the difference in the position [3, 0]:

```
>>> iris_X_prime[3, 0]
5.87923077
>>> iris_X[3, 0]
nan
```

## How it works...

The imputation works by employing different strategies. The default is mean, but in total there are:

▶   mean (default)

▶   median

▶   most_frequent (the mode)

scikit-learn will use the selected strategy to calculate the value for each non-missing value in the dataset. It will then simply fill the missing values.

For example, to redo the iris example with the median strategy, simply reinitialize impute with the new strategy:

```
>>> impute = preprocessing.Imputer(strategy='median')
>>> iris_X_prime = impute.fit_transform(iris_X)
>>> iris_X_prime[:5]
```

```
array([[ 5.1,   3.5,   1.4,   0.2],
       [ 4.9,   3. ,   1.4,   0.2],
       [ 4.7,   3.2,   1.3,   0.2],
       [ 5.8,   3.1,   1.5,   0.2],
       [ 5. ,   3.6,   1.4,   0.2]])
```

If the data is missing values, it might be inherently dirty in other places. For instance, in the example in the preceding *How to do it...* section, np.nan (the default missing value) was used as the missing value, but missing values can be represented in many ways. Consider a situation where missing values are -1. In addition to the strategy to compute the missing value, it's also possible to specify the missing value for the imputer. The default is Nan, which will handle np.nan values.

To see an example of this, modify iris_X to have -1 as the missing value. It sounds crazy, but since the iris dataset contains measurements that are always possible, many people will fill the missing values with -1 to signify they're not there:

```
>>> iris_X[np.isnan(iris_X)] = -1
>>> iris_X[:5]
array([[ 5.1,   3.5,   1.4,   0.2],
       [ 4.9,   3. ,   1.4,   0.2],
       [ 4.7,   3.2,   1.3,   0.2],
       [-1. ,   3.1,   1.5,   0.2],
       [ 5. ,   3.6,   1.4,   0.2]])
```

Filling these in is as simple as the following:

```
>>> impute = preprocessing.Imputer(missing_values=-1)
>>> iris_X_prime = impute.fit_transform(iris_X)
>>> iris_X_prime[:5]
array([[ 5.1        ,   3.5 ,   1.4 ,   0.2 ],
       [ 4.9        ,   3.  ,   1.4 ,   0.2 ],
       [ 4.7        ,   3.2 ,   1.3 ,   0.2 ],
       [ 5.87923077,   3.1 ,   1.5 ,   0.2 ],
       [ 5.        ,   3.6 ,   1.4 ,   0.2 ]])
```

## There's more...

pandas also provides a functionality to fill missing data. It actually might be a bit more flexible, but it is less reusable:

```
>>> import pandas as pd
>>> iris_X[masking_array] = np.nan
>>> iris_df = pd.DataFrame(iris_X, columns=iris.feature_names)
>>> iris_df.fillna(iris_df.mean())['sepal length (cm)'].head(5)
0    5.100000
```

```
1    4.900000
2    4.700000
3    5.879231
4    5.000000
Name: sepal length (cm), dtype: float64
```

To mention its flexibility, `fillna` can be passed any sort of statistic, that is, the strategy is more arbitrarily defined:

```
>>> iris_df.fillna(iris_df.max())['sepal length (cm)'].head(5)
0    5.1
1    4.9
2    4.7
3    7.9
4    5.0
Name: sepal length (cm), dtype: float64
```

# Using Pipelines for multiple preprocessing steps

Pipelines are (at least to me) something I don't think about using often, but are useful. They can be used to tie together many steps into one object. This allows for easier tuning and better access to the configuration of the entire model, not just one of the steps.

## Getting ready

This is the first section where we'll combine multiple data processing steps into a single step. In scikit-learn, this is known as a Pipeline. In this section, we'll first deal with missing data via imputation; however, after that, we'll scale the data to get a mean of zero and a standard deviation of one.

Let's create a dataset that is missing some values, and then we'll look at how to create a Pipeline:

```
>>> from sklearn import datasets
>>> import numpy as np
>>> mat = datasets.make_spd_matrix(10)
>>> masking_array = np.random.binomial(1, .1, mat.shape).astype(bool)
>>> mat[masking_array] = np.nan
>>> mat[:4, :4]
array([[ 0.56716186, -0.20344151,         nan, -0.22579163],
       [        nan,  1.98881836, -2.25445983,  1.27024191],
       [ 0.29327486, -2.25445983,  3.15525425, -1.64685403],
       [-0.22579163,  1.27024191, -1.64685403,  1.32240835]])
```

Great, now we can create a Pipeline.

## How to do it...

Without Pipelines, the process will look something like the following:

```
>>> from sklearn import preprocessing
>>> impute = preprocessing.Imputer()
>>> scaler = preprocessing.StandardScaler()
>>> mat_imputed = impute.fit_transform(mat)
>>> mat_imputed[:4, :4]
array([[ 0.56716186, -0.20344151, -0.80554023, -0.22579163],
       [ 0.04235695,  1.98881836, -2.25445983,  1.27024191],
       [ 0.29327486, -2.25445983,  3.15525425, -1.64685403],
       [-0.22579163,  1.27024191, -1.64685403,  1.32240835]])
>>> mat_imp_and_scaled = scaler.fit_transform(mat_imputed)
array([[  2.235e+00,  -6.291e-01,   1.427e-16,  -7.496e-01],
       [  0.000e+00,   1.158e+00,  -9.309e-01,   9.072e-01],
       [  1.068e+00,  -2.301e+00,   2.545e+00,  -2.323e+00],
       [ -1.142e+00,   5.721e-01,  -5.405e-01,   9.650e-01]])
```

Notice that the prior missing value is 0. This is expected because this value was imputed using the mean strategy, and scaling subtracts the mean.

Now that we've looked at a non-Pipeline example, let's look at how we can incorporate a Pipeline:

```
>>> from sklearn import pipeline
>>> pipe = pipeline.Pipeline([('impute', impute), ('scaler', scaler)])
```

Take a look at the Pipeline. As we can see, Pipeline defines the steps that designate the progression of methods:

```
>>> pipe
Pipeline(steps=[('impute', Imputer(axis=0, copy=True, missing_
values='NaN', strategy='mean', verbose=0)), ('scalar',
StandardScaler(copy=True, with_mean=True, with_std=True))])
```

This is the best part; simply call the `fit_transform` method on the `pipe` object. These separate steps are completed in a single step:

```
>>> new_mat = pipe.fit_transform(mat)
>>> new_mat [:4, :4]
array([[  2.235e+00,  -6.291e-01,   1.427e-16,  -7.496e-01],
       [  0.000e+00,   1.158e+00,  -9.309e-01,   9.072e-01],
       [  1.068e+00,  -2.301e+00,   2.545e+00,  -2.323e+00],
       [ -1.142e+00,   5.721e-01,  -5.405e-01,   9.650e-01]])
```

We can also confirm that the two different methods give the same result:

```
>>> np.array_equal(new_mat, mat_imp_and_scaled)
True
```

Beautiful!

Later in the book, we'll see just how powerful this concept is. It doesn't stop at preprocessing steps. It can easily extend to dimensionality reduction as well, fitting different learning methods. Dimensionality reduction is handled on it's own in the recipe *Reducing dimensionality with PCA*.

## How it works...

As mentioned earlier, almost every scikit-learn has a similar interface. The important ones that allow Pipelines to function are:

- ▸ `fit`
- ▸ `transform`
- ▸ `fit_transform` (a convenience method)

To be specific, if a Pipeline has *N* objects, the first *N-1* objects must implement both `fit` and `transform`, and the *N*th object must implement at least `fit`. If this doesn't happen, an error will be thrown.

Pipeline will work correctly if these conditions are met, but it is still possible that not every method will work properly. For example, `pipe` has a method, `inverse_transform`, which does exactly what the name entails. However, because the impute step doesn't have an `inverse_transform` method, this method call will fail:

```
>>> pipe.inverse_transform(new_mat)
AttributeError: 'Imputer' object has no attribute 'inverse_transform'
```

However, this is possible with the `scalar` object:

```
>>> scaler.inverse_transform(new_mat) [:4, :4]
array([[ 0.567, -0.203, -0.806, -0.226],
       [ 0.042,  1.989, -2.254,  1.27 ],
       [ 0.293, -2.254,  3.155, -1.647],
       [-0.226,  1.27 , -1.647,  1.322]])
```

Once a proper Pipeline is set up, it functions almost exactly how you'd expect. It's a series of `for` loops that fit and transform at each intermediate step, feeding the output to the subsequent transformation.

To conclude this recipe, I'll try to answer the "why?" question. There are two main reasons:

▶ The first reason is **convenience**. The code becomes quite a bit cleaner; instead of calling `fit` and `transform` over and over, it is offloaded to `sklearn`.

▶ The second, and probably the more important, reason is **cross validation**. Models can become very complex. If a single step in Pipeline has tuning parameters, they might need to be tested; with a single step, the code overhead to test the parameters is low. However, five steps with all of their respective parameters can become difficult to test. Pipelines ease a lot of the burden.

# Reducing dimensionality with PCA

Now it's time to take the math up a level! **Principal component analysis** (**PCA**) is the first somewhat advanced technique discussed in this book. While everything else thus far has been simple statistics, PCA will combine statistics and linear algebra to produce a preprocessing step that can help to reduce dimensionality, which can be the enemy of a simple model.

## Getting ready

PCA is a member of the decomposition module of scikit-learn. There are several other decomposition methods available, which will be covered later in this recipe.

Let's use the `iris` dataset, but it's better if you use your own data:

```
>>> from sklearn import datasets
>>> iris = datasets.load_iris()
>>> iris_X = iris.data
```

## How to do it...

First, import the decomposition module:

```
>>> from sklearn import decomposition
```

Next, instantiate a default PCA object:

```
>>> pca = decomposition.PCA()
>>> pca
PCA(copy=True, n_components=None, whiten=False)
```

Compared to other objects in scikit-learn, PCA takes relatively few arguments. Now that the PCA object is created, simply transform the data by calling the `fit_transform` method, with `iris_X` as the argument:

```
>>> iris_pca = pca.fit_transform(iris_X)
>>> iris_pca[:5]
array([[ -2.684e+00,  -3.266e-01,   2.151e-02,   1.006e-03],
       [ -2.715e+00,   1.696e-01,   2.035e-01,   9.960e-02],
       [ -2.890e+00,   1.373e-01,  -2.471e-02,   1.930e-02],
       [ -2.746e+00,   3.111e-01,  -3.767e-02,  -7.596e-02],
       [ -2.729e+00,  -3.339e-01,  -9.623e-02,  -6.313e-02]])
```

Now that the PCA has been fit, we can see how well it has done at explaining the variance (explained in the following *How it works...* section):

```
>>> pca.explained_variance_ratio_
array([ 0.925,  0.053,  0.017,  0.005])
```

## How it works...

PCA has a general mathematic definition and a specific use case in data analysis. PCA finds the set of orthogonal directions that represent the original data matrix.

Generally, PCA works by mapping the original dataset into a new space where the new column vectors of the matrix are each orthogonal. From a data analysis perspective, PCA transforms the covariance matrix of the data into column vectors that can "explain" certain percentages of the variance. For example, with the `iris` dataset, 92.5 percent of the variance of the overall dataset can be explained by the first component.

This is extremely useful because dimensionality is problematic in data analysis. Quite often, algorithms applied to high-dimensional datasets will overfit on the initial training, and thus loose generality to the test set. If most of the underlying structure of the data can be faithfully represented by fewer dimensions, then it's generally considered a worthwhile trade-off.

To demonstrate this, we'll apply the PCA transformation to the `iris` dataset and only include two dimensions. The `iris` dataset can normally be separated quite well using all the dimensions:

```
>>> pca = decomposition.PCA(n_components=2)
>>> iris_X_prime = pca.fit_transform(iris_X)
>>> iris_X_prime.shape
(150, 2)
```

Our data matrix is now 150 x 2, instead of 150 x 4.

The usefulness of two dimensions is that it is now very easy to plot.

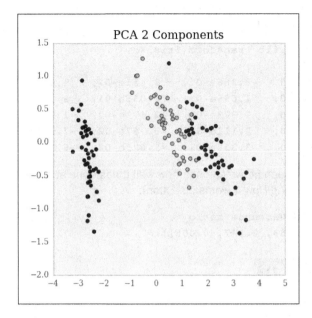

The separability of the classes remain even after reducing the number of dimensionality by two.

We can see how much of the variance is represented by the two components that remain:

```
>>> pca.explained_variance_ratio_.sum()
0.9776
```

## There's more...

The PCA object can also be created with the amount of explained variance in mind from the start. For example, if we want to be able to explain at least 98 percent of the variance, the PCA object will be created as follows:

```
>>> pca = decomposition.PCA(n_components=.98)
>>> iris_X_prime = pca.fit(iris_X)
>>> pca.explained_variance_ratio_.sum()
1.0
```

Since we wanted to explain variance slightly more than the two component examples, a third was included.

# Using factor analysis for decomposition

Factor analysis is another technique we can use to reduce dimensionality. However, factor analysis makes assumptions and PCA does not. The basic assumption is that there are implicit features responsible for the features of the dataset.

This recipe will boil down to the explicit features from our samples in an attempt to understand the independent variables as much as the dependent variables.

## Getting ready

To compare PCA and factor analysis, let's use the `iris` dataset again, but we'll first need to load the factor analysis class:

```
>>> from sklearn.decomposition import FactorAnalysis
```

## How to do it...

From a programming perspective, factor analysis isn't much different from PCA:

```
>>> fa = FactorAnalysis(n_components=2)
>>> iris_two_dim = fa.fit_transform(iris.data)
>>> iris_two_dim[:5]
array([[-1.33125848,  0.55846779],
       [-1.33914102, -0.00509715],
       [-1.40258715, -0.307983  ],
       [-1.29839497, -0.71854288],
       [-1.33587575,  0.36533259]])
```

**Downloading the example code**

You can download the example code files for all Packt books you have purchased from your account at http://www.packtpub.com. If you purchased this book elsewhere, you can visit http://www.packtpub.com/support and register to have the files e-mailed directly to you

Compare the following plot to the plot in the last section:

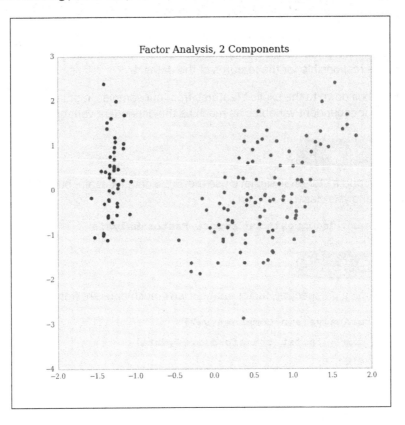

Since factor analysis is a probabilistic transform, we can examine different aspects such as the log likelihood of the observations under the model, and better still, compare the log likelihoods across models.

Factor analysis is not without flaws. The reason is that you're not fitting a model to predict an outcome, you're fitting a model as a preparation step. This isn't a bad thing per se, but errors here compound when training the actual model.

## How it works...

Factor analysis is similar to PCA, which was covered previously. However, there is an important distinction to be made. PCA is a linear transformation of the data to a different space where the first component "explains" the variance of the data, and each subsequent component is orthogonal to the first component.

For example, you can think of PCA as taking a dataset of *N* dimensions and going down to some space of *M* dimensions, where *M* < *N*.

Factor analysis, on the other hand, works under the assumption that there are only *M* important features and a linear combination of these features (plus noise) creates the dataset in *N* dimensions. To put it another way, you don't do regression on an outcome variable, you do regression on the features to determine the latent factors of the dataset.

# Kernel PCA for nonlinear dimensionality reduction

Most of the techniques in statistics are linear by nature, so in order to capture nonlinearity, we might need to apply some transformation. PCA is, of course, a linear transformation. In this recipe, we'll look at applying nonlinear transformations, and then apply PCA for dimensionality reduction.

## Getting ready

Life would be so easy if data was always linearly separable, but unfortunately it's not. Kernel PCA can help to circumvent this issue. Data is first run through the kernel function that projects the data onto a different space; then PCA is performed.

To familiarize yourself with the kernel functions, it will be a good exercise to think of how to generate data that is separable by the kernel functions available in the kernel PCA. Here, we'll do that with the cosine kernel. This recipe will have a bit more theory than the previous recipes.

## How to do it...

The **cosine kernel** works by comparing the angle between two samples represented in the feature space. It is useful when the magnitude of the vector perturbs the typical distance measure used to compare samples.

As a reminder, the cosine between two vectors is given by the following:

$$\cos(\theta) = \frac{A \cdot B}{\|A\| \|B\|}$$

This means that the cosine between A and B is the dot product of the two vectors normalized by the product of the individual norms. The magnitude of vectors A and B have no influence on this calculation.

So, let's generate some data and see how useful it is. First, we'll imagine there are two different underlying processes; we'll call them A and B:

```
>>> import numpy as np
>>> A1_mean = [1, 1]
>>> A1_cov = [[2, .99], [1, 1]]
>>> A1 = np.random.multivariate_normal(A1_mean, A1_cov, 50)

>>> A2_mean = [5, 5]
>>> A2_cov = [[2, .99], [1, 1]]
>>> A2 = np.random.multivariate_normal(A2_mean, A2_cov, 50)

>>> A = np.vstack((A1, A2))

>>> B_mean = [5, 0]
>>> B_cov = [[.5, -1], [-.9, .5]]
>>> B = np.random.multivariate_normal(B_mean, B_cov, 100)
```

Once plotted, it will look like the following:

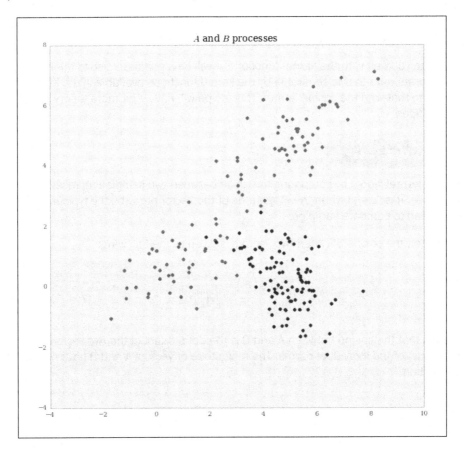

By visual inspection, it seems that the two classes are from different processes, but separating them in one slice might be difficult. So, we'll use the kernel PCA with the cosine kernel discussed earlier:

```
>>> kpca = decomposition.KernelPCA(kernel='cosine', n_components=1)
>>> AB = np.vstack((A, B))
>>> AB_transformed = kpca.fit_transform(AB)
```

Visualized in one dimension after the kernel PCA, the dataset looks like the following:

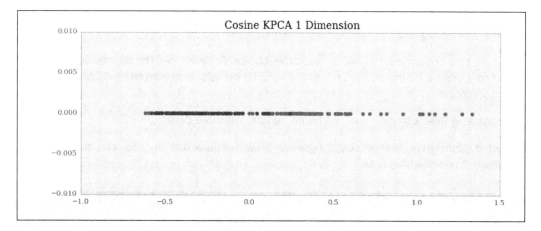

Contrast this with PCA without a kernel:

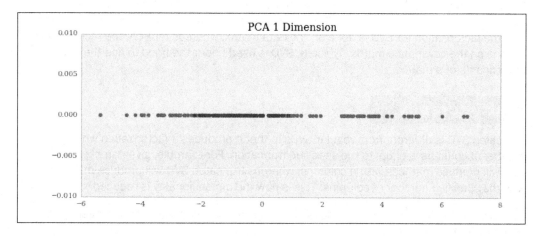

Clearly, the kernel PCA does a much better job.

## How it works...

There are several different kernels available as well as the cosine kernel. You can even write your own kernel function. The available kernels are:

- ▸ `poly` (polynomial)
- ▸ `rbf` (radial basis function)
- ▸ `sigmoid`
- ▸ `cosine`
- ▸ `precomputed`

There are also options contingent of the kernel choice. For example, the degree argument will specify the degree for the `poly`, `rbf`, and `sigmoid` kernels; also, gamma will affect the `rbf` or `poly` kernels.

The recipe on SVM will cover the `rbf` kernel function in more detail.

A word of caution: kernel methods are great to create separability, but they can also cause overfitting if used without care.

# Using truncated SVD to reduce dimensionality

Truncated **Singular Value Decomposition** (**SVD**) is a matrix factorization technique that factors a matrix M into the three matrices U, Σ, and V. This is very similar to PCA, excepting that the factorization for SVD is done on the data matrix, whereas for PCA, the factorization is done on the covariance matrix. Typically, SVD is used under the hood to find the principle components of a matrix.

## Getting ready

Truncated SVD is different from regular SVDs in that it produces a factorization where the number of columns is equal to the specified truncation. For example, given an *n* x *n* matrix, SVD will produce matrices with *n* columns, whereas truncated SVD will produce matrices with the specified number of columns. This is how the dimensionality is reduced.

Here, we'll again use the `iris` dataset so that you can compare this outcome against the PCA outcome:

```
>>> from sklearn.datasets import load_iris
>>> iris = load_iris()
>>> iris_data = iris.data
>>> iris_target = iris.target
```

## How to do it...

This object follows the same form as the other objects we've used. First, we'll import the required object, then we'll fit the model and examine the results:

```
>>> from sklearn.decomposition import TruncatedSVD
>>> svd = TruncatedSVD(2)
>>> iris_transformed = svd.fit_transform(iris_data)
>>> iris_data[:5]
array([[ 5.1,  3.5,  1.4,  0.2],
       [ 4.9,  3. ,  1.4,  0.2],
       [ 4.7,  3.2,  1.3,  0.2],
       [ 4.6,  3.1,  1.5,  0.2],
       [ 5. ,  3.6,  1.4,  0.2]])

>>> iris_transformed[:5]
array([[ 5.91220352, -2.30344211],
       [ 5.57207573, -1.97383104],
       [ 5.4464847 , -2.09653267],
       [ 5.43601924, -1.87168085],
       [ 5.87506555, -2.32934799]])
```

The output will look like the following:

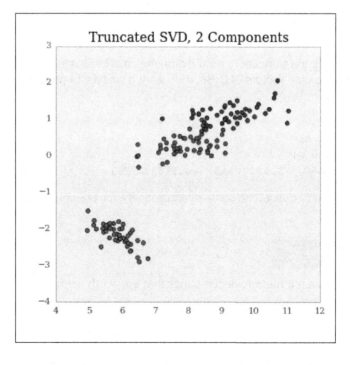

## How it works...

Now that we've walked through how `TruncatedSVD` is performed in scikit-learn, let's look at how we can use only `scipy`, and learn a bit in the process.

First, we need to use `linalg` of `scipy` to perform SVD:

```
>>> from scipy.linalg import svd
>>> D = np.array([[1, 2], [1, 3], [1, 4]])
>>> D
array([[1, 2],
       [1, 3],
       [1, 4]])

>>> U, S, V = svd(D, full_matrices=False)
>>> U.shape, S.shape, V.shape
((3, 2), (2,), (2, 2))
```

We can reconstruct the original matrix D to confirm U, S, and V as a decomposition:

```
>>> np.dot(U.dot(np.diag(S)), V)
array([[1, 2],
       [1, 3],
       [1, 4]])
```

The matrix that is actually returned by `TruncatedSVD` is the dot product of the U and S matrices.

If we want to simulate the truncation, we will drop the smallest singular values and the corresponding column vectors of U. So, if we want a single component here, we do the following:

```
>>> new_S = S[0]
>>> new_U = U[:, 0]
>>> new_U.dot(new_S)
array([-2.20719466, -3.16170819, -4.11622173])
```

In general, if we want to truncate to some dimensionality, for example, *t*, we drop *N-t* singular values.

## There's more...

`TruncatedSVD` has a few miscellaneous things that are worth noting with respect to the method.

## Sign flipping

There's a "gotcha" with truncated SVDs. Depending on the state of the random number generator, successive fittings of `TruncatedSVD` can flip the signs of the output. In order to avoid this, it's advisable to fit `TruncatedSVD` once, and then use transforms from then on. Another good reason for Pipelines!

To carry this out, do the following:

```
>>> tsvd = TruncatedSVD(2)
>>> tsvd.fit(iris_data)
>>> tsvd.transform(iris_data)
```

## Sparse matrices

One advantage of `TruncatedSVD` over PCA is that `TruncatedSVD` can operate on sparse matrices while PCA cannot. This is due to the fact that the covariance matrix must be computed for PCA, which requires operating on the entire matrix.

# Decomposition to classify with DictionaryLearning

In this recipe, we'll show how a decomposition method can actually be used for classification. `DictionaryLearning` attempts to take a dataset and transform it into a sparse representation.

## Getting ready

With `DictionaryLearning`, the idea is that the features are a basis for the resulting datasets. In an effort to keep this recipe short, I'll assume you have `idis_data` and `iris_target` ready to go.

## How to do it...

First, import `DictionaryLearning`:

```
>>> from sklearn.decomposition import DictionaryLearning
```

Next, use three components to represent the three species of `iris`:

```
>>> dl = DictionaryLearning(3)
```

Then transform every other data point so that we can test the classifier on the resulting data points after the learner is trained:

```
>>> transformed = dl.fit_transform(iris_data[::2])
>>> transformed[:5]
array([[ 0.      ,   6.34476574,   0.      ],
       [ 0.      ,   5.83576461,   0.      ],
       [ 0.      ,   6.32038375,   0.      ],
       [ 0.      ,   5.89318572,   0.      ],
       [ 0.      ,   5.45222715,   0.      ]])
```

We can visualize the output. Notice how each value is sited on the x, y, or z axis along with the other values and 0; this is called sparseness.

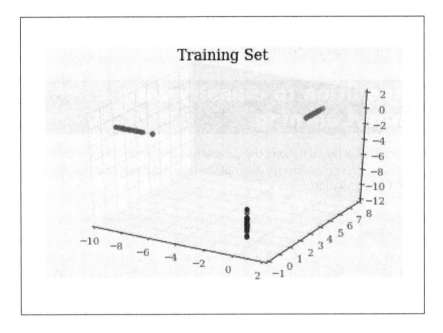

If you look closely, you can see there was some training error. One of the classes was misclassified. Only being wrong once isn't a big deal, though.

Next, let's fit (not `fit_transform`) the testing set:

```
>>> transformed = dl.transform(iris_data[1::2])
```

The following screenshot shows its performance:

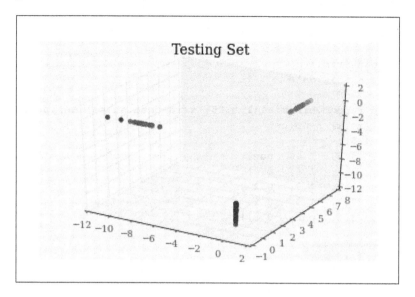

Notice again that there was some error in the classification. If you remember some of the other visualizations, the blue and green classes were the two classes that often appeared close together.

## How it works...

`DictionaryLearning` has a background in signal processing and neurology. The idea is that only few features can be active at any given time. Therefore, `DictionaryLearning` attempts to find a suitable representation for the underlying data, given the constraint that most of the features should be `0`.

# Putting it all together with Pipelines

Now that we've used Pipelines and data transformation techniques, we'll walk through a more complicated example that combines several of the previous recipes into a pipeline.

## Getting ready

In this section, we'll show off some more of Pipeline's power. When we used it earlier to impute missing values, it was only a quick taste; we'll chain together multiple preprocessing steps to show how Pipelines can remove extra work.

Let's briefly load the `iris` dataset and seed it with some missing values:

```
>>> from sklearn.datasets import load_iris
>>> import numpy as np

>>> iris = load_iris()
>>> iris_data = iris.data

>>> mask = np.random.binomial(1, .25, iris_data.shape).astype(bool)
>>> iris_data[mask] = np.nan
>>> iris_data[:5]
array([[ 5.1,  3.5,  1.4,  nan],
       [ nan,  3. ,  1.4,  0.2],
       [ 4.7,  3.2,  1.3,  0.2],
       [ 4.6,  3.1,  1.5,  0.2],
       [ 5. ,  3.6,  nan,  0.2]])
```

## How to do it...

The goal of this chapter is to first impute the missing values of `iris_data`, and then perform PCA on the corrected dataset. You can imagine (and we'll do it later) that this workflow might need to be split between a training dataset and a holdout set; Pipelines will make this easier, but first we need to take a baby step.

Let's load the required libraries:

```
>>> from sklearn import pipeline, preprocessing, decomposition
```

Next, create the imputer and PCA classes:

```
>>> pca = decomposition.PCA()
>>> imputer = preprocessing.Imputer()
```

Now that we have the classes we need, we can load them into Pipeline:

```
>>> pipe = pipeline.Pipeline([('imputer', imputer), ('pca', pca)])
>>> iris_data_transformed = pipe.fit_transform(iris_data)
>>> iris_data_transformed[:5]
array([[ -2.42e+00,  -3.59e-01,  -6.88e-01,  -3.49e-01],
       [ -2.44e+00,  -6.94e-01,   3.27e-01,   4.87e-01],
       [ -2.94e+00,   2.45e-01,  -1.85e-03,   4.37e-02],
       [ -2.79e+00,   4.29e-01,  -8.05e-03,   9.65e-02],
       [ -6.46e-01,   8.87e-01,   7.54e-01,  -5.19e-01]])
```

This takes a lot more management if we use separate steps. Instead of each step requiring a fit transform, this step is performed only once. Not to mention that we only have to keep track of one object!

## How it works...

Hopefully it was obvious, but each step in Pipeline is passed to a Pipeline object via a list of tuples, with the first element getting the name and the second getting the actual object.

Under the hood, these steps are looped through when a method such as `fit_transform` is called on the Pipeline object.

This said, there are quick and dirty ways to create Pipeline, much in the same way there was a quick way to perform scaling, though we can use `StandardScaler` if we want more power. The `pipeline` function will automatically create the names for the Pipeline objects:

```
>>> pipe2 = pipeline.make_pipeline(imputer, pca)
>>> pipe2.steps
[('imputer', Imputer(axis=0, copy=True, missing_values='NaN',
strategy='mean', verbose=0)),
('pca', PCA(copy=True, n_components=None, whiten=False))]
```

This is the same object that was created in the more verbose method:

```
>>> iris_data_transformed2 = pipe2.fit_transform(iris_data)
>>> iris_data_transformed2[:5]
array([[ -2.42e+00,   -3.59e-01,   -6.88e-01,   -3.49e-01],
       [ -2.44e+00,   -6.94e-01,    3.27e-01,    4.87e-01],
       [ -2.94e+00,    2.45e-01,   -1.85e-03,    4.37e-02],
       [ -2.79e+00,    4.29e-01,   -8.05e-03,    9.65e-02],
       [ -6.46e-01,    8.87e-01,    7.54e-01,   -5.19e-01]])
```

## There's more...

We just walked through Pipelines at a very high level, but it's unlikely that we will want to apply the base transformation. Therefore, the attributes of each object in Pipeline can be accessed from a `set_params` method, where the parameter follows the <parameter's_name>__<parameter's_parameter> convention. For example, let's change the `pca` object to use two components:

```
>>> pipe2.set_params(pca_n_components=2)
Pipeline(steps=[('imputer', Imputer(axis=0, copy=True,
       missing_values='NaN', strategy='mean', verbose=0)),
       ('pca', PCA(copy=True, n_components=2, whiten=False))])
```

The __ notation is pronounced as **dunder** in the Python community.

Notice `n_components=2` in the preceding output. Just as a test, we can output the same transformation we already did twice, and the output will be an *N x 2* matrix:

```
>>> iris_data_transformed3 = pipe2.fit_transform(iris_data)
>>> iris_data_transformed3[:5]
array([[-2.42, -0.36],
       [-2.44, -0.69],
       [-2.94,  0.24],
       [-2.79,  0.43],
       [-0.65,  0.89]])
```

# Using Gaussian processes for regression

In this recipe, we'll use the **Gaussian process** for regression. In the linear models section, we saw how representing prior information on the coefficients was possible using **Bayesian Ridge Regression**.

With a Gaussian process, it's about the variance and not the mean. However, with a Gaussian process, we assume the mean is 0, so it's the covariance function we'll need to specify.

The basic setup is similar to how a prior can be put on the coefficients in a typical regression problem. With a GP, a prior can be put on the functional form of the data, and it's the covariance between the data points that is used to model the data, and therefore, must be fit from the data.

## Getting ready

So, let's use some regression data and walkthrough how Gaussian processes work in scikit-learn:

```
>>> from sklearn.datasets import load_boston
>>> boston = load_boston()

>>> boston_X = boston.data
>>> boston_y = boston.target

>>> train_set = np.random.choice([True, False], len(boston_y),
                                  p=[.75, .25])
```

## How to do it...

Now that we have the data, we'll create a scikit-learn `GaussianProcess` object. By default, it uses a constant regression function and squared exponential correlation, which is one of the more common choices:

```
>>> from sklearn.gaussian_process import GaussianProcess
>>> gp = GaussianProcess()
>>> gp.fit(boston_X[train_set], boston_y[train_set])
GaussianProcess(beta0=None, corr=<function squared_exponential
                at 0x110809488>, normalize=True,
                nugget=array(2.220446049250313e-15),
                optimizer='fmin_cobyla', random_start=1,
                random_state=<mtrand.RandomState object
                at 0x10b9b58b8>, regr=<function constant
                at 0x1108090c8>, storage_mode='full',
                theta0=array([[ 0.1]]), thetaL=None, thetaU=None,
                verbose=False)
```

That's a formidable object definition. The following are a couple of things to point out:

- ► `beta0`: This is the regression weight. This defaults in a way such that MLE is used for estimation.

- ► `corr`: This is the correlation function. There are several built-in correlation functions. We'll look at more of them in the following *How it works...* section.

- ► `regr`: This is the constant regression function.

- ► `nugget`: This is the regularization parameter. It defaults to a very small number. You can either pass one value to be used for each data point or a single value that needs to be applied uniformly.

- ► `normalize`: This defaults to `True`, and it will center and scale the features. This would be scale is R.

Okay, so now that we fit the object, let's look at it's performance against the test object:

```
>>> test_preds = gp.predict(boston_X[~train_set])
```

Let's plot the predicted values versus the actual values; then, because we're doing regression, it's probably a good idea to look at plotted residuals and a histogram of the residuals:

```
>>> from matplotlib import pyplot as plt
>>> f, ax = plt.subplots(figsize=(10, 7), nrows=3)
>>> f.tight_layout()

>>> ax[0].plot(range(len(test_preds)), test_preds,
               label='Predicted Values');
>>> ax[0].plot(range(len(test_preds)), boston_y[~train_set],
               label='Actual Values');
>>> ax[0].set_title("Predicted vs Actuals")
>>> ax[0].legend(loc='best')

>>> ax[1].plot(range(len(test_preds)),
               test_preds - boston_y[~train_set]);
>>> ax[1].set_title("Plotted Residuals")

>>> ax[2].hist(test_preds - boston_y[~train_set]);
>>> ax[2].set_title("Histogram of Residuals")
```

The output is as follows:

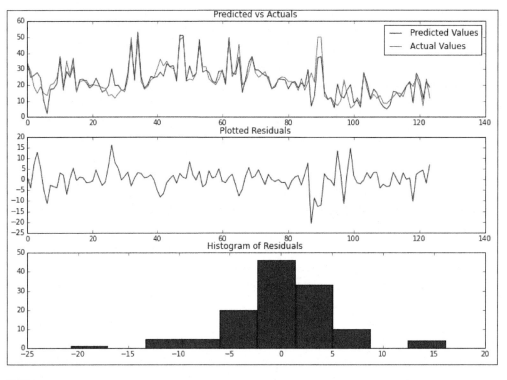

## How it works...

Now that we've worked through a very quick example, let's look a little more at what some of the parameters do and how we can tune them based on the model we're trying to fit.

First, let's try to understand what's going on with the `corr` function. This function describes the relationship between the different pairs of X. The following five different correlation functions are offered by scikit-learn:

- `absolute_exponential`
- `squared_exponential`
- `generalized_exponential`
- `cubic`
- `linear`

For example, the squared exponential has the following form:

$$K = \backslash \exp\left(-\left\{\backslash frac\left\{|d|^{\wedge} 2\right\}\left\{2l^{\wedge}2\right\}\right\}\right)$$

Linear, on the other hand, is just the dot product of the two points in question:

$$K = x^{\wedge}Tx^{\wedge}\left\{'\right\}$$

Another parameter of interest is `theta0`. This represents the starting point in the estimation of the the parameters.

Once we have an estimation of K and the mean, the process is fully specified due to it being a Gaussian process; emphasis is put on Gaussian, a reason it's so popular for general machine learning work.

Let's use a different `regr` function, apply a different `theta0`, and look at how the predictions differ:

```
>>> gp = GaussianProcess(regr='linear', theta0=5e-1)
>>> gp.fit(boston_X[train_set], boston_y[train_set]);
>>> linear_preds = gp.predict(boston_X[~train_set])
>>> f, ax = plt.subplots(figsize=(7, 5))
```

Let's have a look at the fit:

```
>>> f.tight_layout()
```

```
>>> ax.hist(test_preds - boston_y[~train_set],
```

```
            label='Residuals Original', color='b', alpha=.5);
>>> ax.hist(linear_preds - boston_y[~train_set],
            label='Residuals Linear', color='r', alpha=.5);
>>> ax.set_title("Residuals")
>>> ax.legend(loc='best')
```

The following is the output:

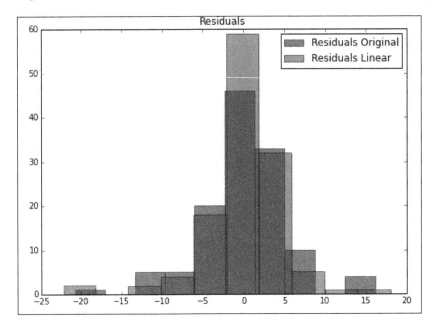

Clearly, the second model's predictions are slightly better for the most part. If we want to sum this up, we can look at the MSE of the predictions:

```
>>> np.power(test_preds - boston_y[~train_set], 2).mean()
26.254844099612455
>>> np.power(linear_preds - boston_y[~train_set], 2).mean()
21.938924337056068
```

## There's more...

We might want to understand the uncertainty in our estimates. When we make the predictions, if we pass the `eval_MSE` argument as `True`, we'll get MSE and the predicted values. From a mechanics standpoint, a tuple of predictions and MSE is returned:

```
>>> test_preds, MSE = gp.predict(boston_X[~train_set], eval_MSE=True)
>>> MSE[:5]
array([ 11.95314572,    8.48397825,    6.0287539 ,   29.20844347,
         0.36427829])
```

So, now that we have errors in the estimates (unfortunately), let's plot the first few to get an indication of accuracy:

```
>>> f, ax = plt.subplots(figsize=(7, 5))

>>> n = 20
>>> rng = range(n)
>>> ax.scatter(rng, test_preds[:n])
>>> ax.errorbar(rng, test_preds[:n], yerr=1.96*MSE[:n])

>>> ax.set_title("Predictions with Error Bars")

>>> ax.set_xlim((-1, 21));
```

The following is the output:

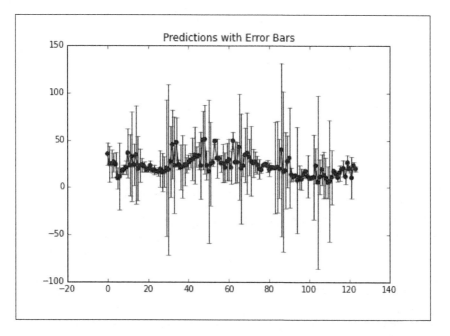

As you can see, there's quite a bit of variance in the estimates for a lot of these points. On the other hand, our overall error wasn't too bad.

# Defining the Gaussian process object directly

We just touched the surface of Gaussian processes. In this recipe, we'll look at how we can directly access the Gaussian process object with the correlation function we want.

## Getting ready

Within the `gaussian_process` module, there is direct access to many of the correlation functions or regression functions. This means that instead of creating the `GaussianProcess` object, we can just create this object through a function. If you're more familiar with object-oriented code, this is basically a class method at the module level.

In this chapter, we'll march through most of the functions and show their results on example data. Do not stop at these examples if you want to get more familiar with the behavior of the various covariate functions. Hopefully, you're still using IPython (or the notebook).

Since this doesn't expose anything thing new mathematically, we'll just show how to do it.

## How to do it...

First, we'll import some basic regression data:

```
>>> from sklearn.datasets import make_regression
>>> X, y = make_regression(1000, 1, 1)
>>> from sklearn.gaussian_process import regression_models
```

First up is the constant correlation function. This will comprise a constant and more for completeness:

```
>>> regression_models.constant(X)[:5]
array([[ 1.],
       [ 1.],
       [ 1.],
       [ 1.],
       [ 1.]])
```

Another option is the squared exponential correlation function. This is also the default for the `GaussianProcess` class:

```
>>> regression_models.linear(X)[:1]
array([[ 1., 0.38833572]])

>>> regression_models.quadratic(X)[:1]
array([[ 1., 0.38833572, 0.15080463]])
```

## How it works...

Now that we have the regression function, we can feed it directly into the `GaussianProcess` object. The default is the constant regression function, but we can just as easily pass it in a linear model or a quadratic model.

# Using stochastic gradient descent for regression

In this recipe, we'll get our first taste of stochastic gradient descent. We'll use it for regression here, but for the next recipe, we'll use it for classification.

## Getting ready

**Stochastic Gradient Descent** (**SGD**) is often an unsung hero in machine learning. Underneath many algorithms, there is SGD doing the work. It's popular due to its simplicity and speed—these are both very good things to have when dealing with a lot of data.

The other nice thing about SGD is that while it's at the core of many ML algorithms computationally, it does so because it easily describes the process. At the end of the day, we apply some transformation on the data, and then we fit our data to the model with some loss function.

## How to do it...

If SGD is good on large datasets, we should probably test it on a fairly large dataset:

```
>>> from sklearn import datasets
>>> X, y = datasets.make_regression(int(1e6))
# Just in case the 1e6 throws you off.
>>> print "{:,}".format(int(1e6))
1,000,000
```

It's probably worth gaining some intuition about the composition and size of the object. Thankfully, we're dealing with NumPy arrays, so we can just access `nbytes`. The built-in Python way to access the object size doesn't work for NumPy arrays. This output be system dependent, so you may not get the same results:

```
>>> print "{:,}".format(X.nbytes)
800,000,000
```

To get some human perspective, we can convert `nbytes` to megabytes. There are roughly 1 million bytes in an MB:

```
>>> X.nbytes / 1e6
800.0
```

So, the number of bytes per data point is:

```
>>> X.nbytes / (X.shape[0]*X.shape[1])
8
```

Well, isn't that tidy, and fairly tangential, for what we're trying to accomplish; however, it's worth knowing how to get the size of the objects you're dealing with.

So, now that we have the data, we can simply fit a `SGDRegressor` model:

```
>>> from sklearn import linear_model
>>> sgd = linear_model.SGDRegressor()
>>> train = np.random.choice([True, False], size=len(y), p=[.75, .25])
>>> sgd.fit(X[train], y[train])
SGDRegressor(alpha=0.0001, epsilon=0.1, eta0=0.01,
            fit_intercept=True, l1_ratio=0.15,
            learning_rate='invscaling', loss='squared_loss',
            n_iter=5, penalty='l2', power_t=0.25, random_state=None,
            shuffle=False, verbose=0, warm_start=False)
```

So, we have another "beefy" object. The main thing to know now is that our loss function is `squared_loss`, which is the same thing that occurs during linear regression. Also worth noting is that shuffle will generate a random shuffle of the data. This is useful if you want to break a potentially spurious correlation. With `fit_intercept`, scikit-learn will automatically include a column of ones. If you like to see more through the output of the fitting, set `verbose` to 1.

We can then predict, as we previously have, using scikit-learn's consistent API:

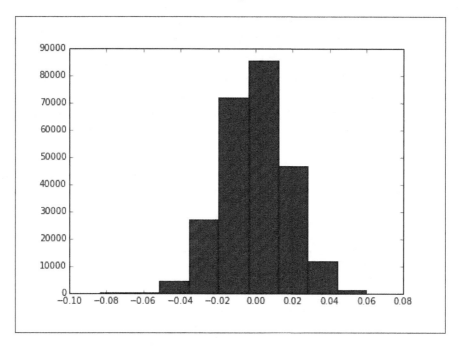

You can see we actually got a really good fit. There is barely any variation and the histogram has a nice normal look.

## How it works...

Clearly, the fake dataset we used wasn't too bad, but you can imagine datasets with larger magnitudes. For example, if you worked in Wall Street on any given day, there might be two billion transactions on any given exchange in a market. Now, imagine that you have a week's or year's data. Running in-core algorithms does not work with huge volumes of data.

The reason this is normally difficult is that to do standard gradient descent, we're required to calculate the gradient at every step. The gradient has the standard definition from any third calculus course.

The gist of the algorithm is that at each step we calculate a new set of coefficients and update this by a learning rate and the outcome of the objective function.

In pseudo code, this might look like the following:

```
>>> while not_converged:
        w = w - learning_rate*gradient(cost(w))
```

The relevant variables are as follows:

- ▶ `w`: This is the coefficient matrix.
- ▶ `learning_rate`: This shows how big a step to take at each iteration. This might be important to tune if you aren't getting a good convergence.
- ▶ `gradient`: This is the matrix of second derivatives.
- ▶ `cost`: This is the squared error for regression. We'll see later that this cost function can be adapted to work with classification tasks. This flexibility is one thing that makes SGD so useful.

This will not be so bad, except for the fact that the gradient function is expensive. As the vector of coefficients gets larger, calculating the gradient becomes very expensive. For each update step, we need to calculate a new weight for every point in the data, and then update.

The stochastic gradient descent works slightly differently; instead of the previous definition for batch gradient descent, we'll update the parameter with each new data point. This data point is picked at random, and hence the name stochastic gradient descent.

# 2
# Working with Linear Models

In this chapter, we will cover the following topics:

- ▸ Fitting a line through data
- ▸ Evaluating the linear regression model
- ▸ Using ridge regression to overcome linear regression's shortfalls
- ▸ Optimizing the ridge regression parameter
- ▸ Using sparsity to regularize models
- ▸ Taking a more fundamental approach to regularization with LARS
- ▸ Using linear methods for classification – logistic regression
- ▸ Directly applying Bayesian ridge regression
- ▸ Using boosting to learn from errors

## Introduction

Linear models are fundamental in statistics and machine learning. Many methods rely on a linear combination of variables to describe the relationship in the data. Quite often, great efforts are taken in an attempt to make the transformations necessary so that the data can be described in a linear combination.

In this chapter, we build up from the simplest idea of fitting a straight line through data to classification, and finally to Bayesian ridge regression.

# Fitting a line through data

Now, we get to do some modeling! It's best to start simple; therefore, we'll look at linear regression first. **Linear regression** is the first, and therefore, probably the most fundamental model—a straight line through data.

## Getting ready

The `boston` dataset is perfect to play around with regression. The `boston` dataset has the median home price of several areas in Boston. It also has other factors that might impact housing prices, for example, crime rate.

First, import the `datasets` model, then we can load the dataset:

```
>>> from sklearn import datasets
>>> boston = datasets.load_boston()
```

## How to do it...

Actually, using linear regression in scikit-learn is quite simple. The API for linear regression is basically the same API you're now familiar with from the previous chapter.

First, import the `LinearRegression` object and create an object:

```
>>> from sklearn.linear_model import LinearRegression
>>> lr = LinearRegression()
```

Now, it's as easy as passing the independent and dependent variables to the fit method of `LinearRegression`:

```
>>> lr.fit(boston.data, boston.target)
LinearRegression(copy_X=True, fit_intercept=True, normalize=False)
```

Now, to get the predictions, do the following:

```
>>> predictions = lr.predict(boston.data)
```

It's then probably a good idea to look at how close the predictions are to the actual data. We can use a histogram to look at the differences. These are called the **residuals**, as shown:

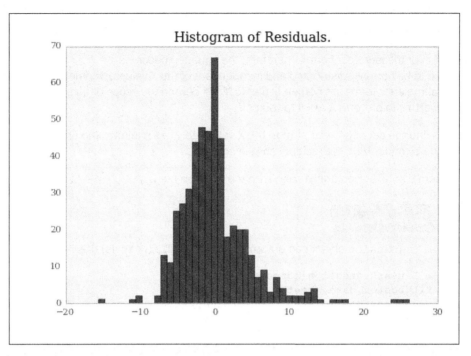

Let's take a look at the coefficients:

```
>>> lr.coef_
array([ -1.07170557e-01,   4.63952195e-02, 2.08602395e-02,
         2.68856140e+00,  -1.77957587e+01, 3.80475246e+00,
         7.51061703e-04,  -1.47575880e+00, 3.05655038e-01,
        -1.23293463e-02,  -9.53463555e-01, 9.39251272e-03,
        -5.25466633e-01])
```

> A common pattern to express the coefficients of the features and their names is `zip(boston.feature_names, lr.coef_)`.

So, going back to the data, we can see which factors have a negative relationship with the outcome, and also the factors that have a positive relationship. For example, and as expected, an increase in the per capita crime rate by town has a negative relationship with the price of a home in Boston. The per capita crime rate is the first coefficient in the regression.

## How it works...

The basic idea of linear regression is to find the set of coefficients of $\beta$ that satisfy $y = X\beta$, where $X$ is the data matrix. It's unlikely that for the given values of $X$, we will find a set of coefficients that exactly satisfy the equation; an error term gets added if there is an inexact specification or measurement error. Therefore, the equation becomes $y = X\beta + \varepsilon$, where $\varepsilon$ is assumed to be normally distributed and independent of the $X$ values. Geometrically, this means that the error terms are perpendicular to $X$. It's beyond the scope of this book, but it might be worth it to prove $E(X\varepsilon) = 0$ to yourself.

In order to find the set of betas that map the $X$ values to $y$, we minimize the error term. This is done by minimizing the residual sum of squares.

This problem can be solved analytically, with the solution being $\beta = (X^T X)^{-1} X^T \hat{y}$.

## There's more...

The `LinearRegression` object can automatically normalize (or scale) the inputs:

```
>>> lr2 = LinearRegression(normalize=True)
>>> lr2.fit(boston.data, boston.target)
LinearRegression(copy_X=True, fit_intercept=True, normalize=True)
>>> predictions2 = lr2.predict(boston.data)
```

# Evaluating the linear regression model

In this recipe, we'll look at how well our regression fits the underlying data. We fit a regression in the last recipe, but didn't pay much attention to how well we actually did it. The first question after we fit the model was clearly *"How well does the model fit?"* In this recipe, we'll examine this question.

## Getting ready

Let's use the `lr` object and `boston` dataset—reach back into your code from the *Fitting a line through data* recipe. The `lr` object will have a lot of useful methods now that the model has been fit.

## How to do it...

There are some very simple metrics and plots we'll want to look at as well. Let's take another look at the residual plot from the last chapter:

```
>>> import matplotlib.pyplot as plt
>>> import numpy as np
```

```
>>> f = plt.figure(figsize=(7, 5))
>>> ax = f.add_subplot(111)
>>> ax.hist(boston.target - predictions, bins=50)
>>> ax.set_title("Histogram of Residuals.")
```

If you're using IPython Notebook, use the `%matplotlib inline` command to render the plots inline. If you're using a regular interpreter, simply type `f.savefig('myfig.png')` and the plot will be saved for you.

 Plotting is done via `matplotlib`. This isn't the focus of this book, but it's useful to plot your results, so we'll show some basic plotting.

The following is the histogram showing the output:

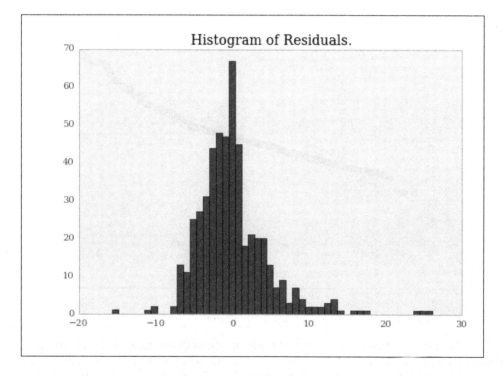

Like I mentioned previously, the error terms should be normal, with a mean of 0. The residuals are the errors; therefore, this plot should be approximately normal. Visually, it's a good fit, though a bit skewed. We can also look at the mean of the residuals, which should be very close to 0:

```
>>> np.mean(boston.target - predictions)
4.3250427394093058e-15
```

Clearly, we are very close.

Another plot worth looking at is a **Q-Q plot**. We'll use **SciPy** here because it has a built-in probability plot:

```
>>> from scipy.stats import probplot
>>> f = plt.figure(figsize=(7, 5))
>>> ax = f.add_subplot(111)
>>> probplot(boston.target - predictions, plot=ax)
```

The following screenshot shows the probability plot:

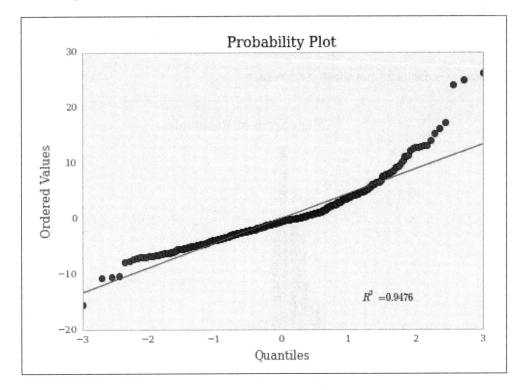

Here, the skewed values we saw earlier are a bit clearer.

We can also look at some other metrics of the fit; **mean squared error** (**MSE**) and **mean absolute deviation** (**MAD**) are two common metrics. Let's define each one in Python and use them. Later in the book, we'll look at how scikit-learn has built-in metrics to evaluate the regression models:

```
>>> def MSE(target, predictions):
        squared_deviation = np.power(target - predictions, 2)
        return np.mean(squared_deviation)
```

```
>>> MSE(boston.target, predictions)
21.897779217687496

>>> def MAD(target, predictions):
        absolute_deviation = np.abs(target - predictions)
        return np.mean(absolute_deviation)

>>> MAD(boston.target, predictions)
3.2729446379969396
```

## How it works...

The formula for MSE is very simple:

$$E\left(\hat{y}_t - y_i\right)^2$$

It takes each predicted value's deviance from the actual value, squares it, and then averages all the squared terms. This is actually what we optimized to find the best set of coefficients for linear regression. The **Gauss-Markov** theorem actually guarantees that the solution to linear regression is the best in the sense that the coefficients have the smallest expected squared error and are unbiased. In the *Using ridge regression to overcome linear regression's shortfalls* recipe, we'll look at what happens when we're okay with our coefficients being biased.

MAD is the expected error for the absolute errors:

$$E\left|\hat{y}_t - y_i\right|$$

MAD isn't used when fitting the linear regression, but it's worth taking a look at. Why? Think about what each one is doing and which errors are more important in each case. For example, with MSE, the larger errors get penalized more than the other terms because of the square term.

## There's more...

One thing that's been glossed over a bit is the fact that the coefficients themselves are random variables, and therefore, they have a distribution. Let's use bootstrapping to look at the distribution of the coefficient for the crime rate. Bootstrapping is a very common technique to get an understanding of the uncertainty of an estimate:

```
>>> n_bootstraps = 1000
>>> len_boston = len(boston.target)
>>> subsample_size = np.int(0.5*len_boston)
```

```
>>> subsample = lambda: np.random.choice(np.arange(0, len_boston),
            size=subsample_size)

>>> coefs = np.ones(n_bootstraps) #pre-allocate the space for the coefs

>>> for i in range(n_bootstraps):
        subsample_idx = subsample()
        subsample_X = boston.data[subsample_idx]
        subsample_y = boston.target[subsample_idx]

>>> lr.fit(subsample_X, subsample_y)

>>> coefs[i] = lr.coef_[0]
```

Now, we can look at the distribution of the coefficient:

```
>>> import matplotlib.pyplot as plt
>>> f = plt.figure(figsize=(7, 5))
>>> ax = f.add_subplot(111)
>>> ax.hist(coefs, bins=50)
>>> ax.set_title("Histogram of the lr.coef_[0].")
```

The following is the histogram that gets generated:

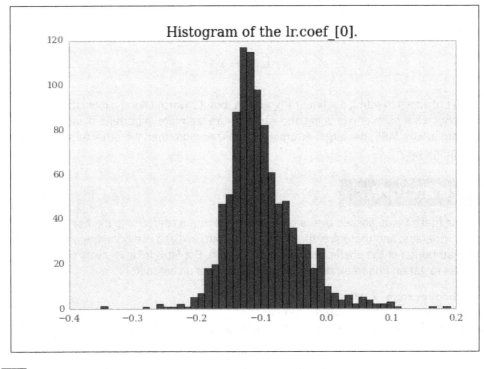

We might also want to look at the bootstrapped confidence interval:

```
>>> np.percentile(coefs, [2.5, 97.5])
array([-0.18566145,  0.03142513])
```

This is interesting; there's actually reason to believe that the crime rate might not have an impact on the home prices. Notice how zero is within CI, which means that it may not play a role.

It's also worth pointing out that bootstrapping can lead to a potentially better estimation for coefficients because the bootstrapped mean with converge to the true mean is faster than the coefficient found using regular estimation when in the limit.

# Using ridge regression to overcome linear regression's shortfalls

In this recipe, we'll learn about ridge regression. It is different from vanilla linear regression; it introduces a regularization parameter to "shrink" the coefficients. This is useful when the dataset has collinear factors.

## Getting ready

Let's load a dataset that has a low effective rank and compare ridge regression with linear regression by way of the coefficients. If you're not familiar with rank, it's the smaller of the linearly independent columns and the linearly independent rows. One of the assumptions of linear regression is that the data matrix is of "full rank".

## How to do it...

First, use `make_regression` to create a simple dataset with three predictors, but an effective rank of 2. **Effective rank** means that while technically the matrix is of full rank, many of the columns have a high degree of colinearity:

```
>>> from sklearn.datasets import make_regression
>>> reg_data, reg_target = make_regression(n_samples=2000,
                        n_features=3, effective_rank=2, noise=10)
```

First, let's take a look at regular linear regression:

```
>>> import numpy as np
>>> n_bootstraps = 1000
>>> len_data = len(reg_data)
>>> subsample_size = np.int(0.75*len_data)
>>> subsample = lambda: np.random.choice(np.arange(0, len_data),
                        size=subsample_size)
```

```
>>> coefs = np.ones((n_bootstraps, 3))

>>> for i in range(n_bootstraps):
        subsample_idx = subsample()
        subsample_X = reg_data[subsample_idx]
        subsample_y = reg_target[subsample_idx]

>>> lr.fit(subsample_X, subsample_y)

>>> coefs[i][0] = lr.coef_[0]
>>> coefs[i][1] = lr.coef_[1]
>>> coefs[i][2] = lr.coef_[2]
```

The following is the output that gets generated:

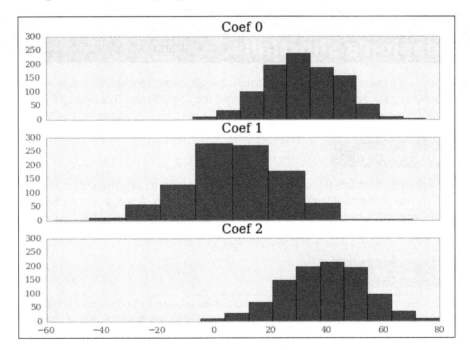

Follow the same procedure with `Ridge`, and have a look at the output:

```
>>> r = Ridge()
>>> n_bootstraps = 1000
>>> len_data = len(reg_data)
>>> subsample_size = np.int(0.75*len_data)
>>> subsample = lambda: np.random.choice(np.arange(0, len_data),
    size=subsample_size)

coefs_r = np.ones((n_bootstraps, 3))
# carry out the same procedure from above
```

The following is the output that gets generated:

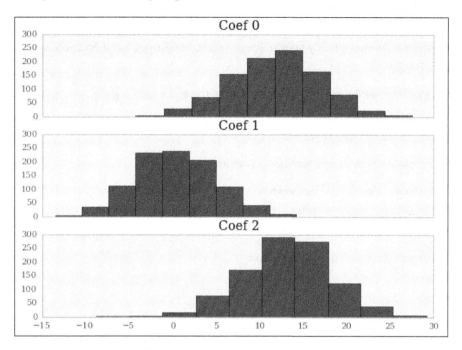

Don't let the similar width of the plots fool you; the coefficients for ridge regression are much closer to 0. Let's look at the average spread between the coefficients:

```
>>> np.mean(coefs - coefs_r, axis=0)
#coefs_r stores the ridge regression coefficients
array([ 22.19529525,  49.54961002,   8.27708536])
```

So, on an average, the coefficients for linear regression are much higher than the ridge regression coefficients. This difference is the bias in the coefficients (forgetting, for a second, the potential bias of the linear regression coefficients). So then, what is the advantage of ridge regression? Well, let's look at the variance of our coefficients:

```
>>> np.var(coefs, axis=0)
array([ 184.50845658,  150.16268077,  263.39096391])


>>> np.var(coefs_r, axis=0)
array([ 21.35161646,  23.95273241,  17.34020101])
```

The variance has been dramatically reduced. This is the bias-variance trade-off that is so often discussed in machine learning. The next recipe will introduce how to tune the regularization parameter in ridge regression, which is at the heart of this trade-off.

## How it works...

Speaking of the regularization parameter, let's go through how ridge regression differs from linear regression. As was already shown, linear regression works, but it finds the vector of betas that minimize $\left\| \hat{y} - X\beta \right\|^2$.

Ridge regression finds the vector of betas that minimize $\left\| \hat{y} - X\beta \right\|^2 + \left\| \Gamma X \right\|^2$.

$\Gamma$ is typically $aI$, or it's some scalar times the identity matrix. We actually used the default alpha when initializing ridge regression.

Now that we created the object, we can look at its attributes:

```
>>> r #notice the alpha parameter
Ridge(alpha=1.0, copy_X=True, fit_intercept=True, max_iter=None,
      normalize=False, solver='auto', tol=0.001)
```

This minimization has the following solution:

$$\beta = \left( X^T X + \Gamma^T \Gamma \right)^{-1} Xy$$

The previous solution is the same as linear regression, except for the $\Gamma^T \Gamma$ term. For a matrix $A$, $AA^T$ is symmetric, and thus positive semidefinite. So, thinking about the translation of matrix algebra from scalar algebra, we effectively divide by a larger number. Multiplication by an inverse is analogous to division. So, this is what squeezes the coefficients towards 0. This is a bit of a crude explanation; for a deeper understanding, you should look at the connections between SVD and ridge regression.

# Optimizing the ridge regression parameter

Once you start using ridge regression to make predictions or learn about relationships in the system you're modeling, you'll start thinking about the choice of alpha.

For example, using OLS regression might show some relationship between two variables; however, when regularized by some alpha, the relationship is no longer significant. This can be a matter of whether a decision needs to be taken.

## Getting ready

This is the first recipe where we'll tune the parameters for a model. This is typically done by cross-validation. There will be recipes laying out a more general way to do this in later recipes, but here we'll walkthrough to be able to tune ridge regression.

If you remember, in ridge regression, the gamma parameter is typically represented as alpha in scikit-learn when calling `RidgeRegression`; so, the question that arises is what the best alpha is. Create a regression dataset, and then let's get started:

```
>>> from sklearn.datasets import make_regression
>>> reg_data, reg_target = make_regression(n_samples=100,
                         n_features=2, effective_rank=1, noise=10)
```

## How to do it...

In the `linear_models` module, there is an object called `RidgeCV`, which stands for **ridge cross-validation**. This performs a cross-validation similar to **leave-one-out cross-validation** (**LOOCV**).

Under the hood, it's going to train the model for all samples except one. It'll then evaluate the error in predicting this one test case:

```
>>> from sklearn.linear_model import RidgeCV
>>> rcv = RidgeCV(alphas=np.array([.1, .2, .3, .4]))
>>> rcv.fit(reg_data, reg_target)
RidgeCV(alphas=array([ 0.1, 0.2, 0.3, 0.4]), cv=None,
        fit_intercept=True, gcv_mode=None, loss_func=None,
        normalize=False, score_func=None, scoring=None,
        store_cv_values=False)
```

After we fit the regression, the `alpha` attribute will be the *best* alpha choice:

```
>>> rcv.alpha_
0.10000000000000001
```

In the previous example, it was the first choice. We might want to hone in on something around .1:

```
>>> rcv2 = RidgeCV(alphas=np.array([.08, .09, .1, .11, .12]))
>>> rcv2.fit(reg_data, reg_target)
RidgeCV(alphas=array([ 0.08,  0.09,  0.1 ,  0.11,  0.12]), cv=None,
                    fit_intercept=True, gcv_mode=None,
                    loss_func=None, normalize=False,
                    score_func=None, scoring=None,
                    store_cv_values=False)

>>> rcv2.alpha_
0.08
```

We can continue this hunt, but hopefully, the mechanics are clear.

## How it works...

The mechanics might be clear, but we should talk a little more about the why and define what was meant by "best". At each step in the cross-validation process, the model scores an error against the test sample. By default, it's essentially a squared error. Check out the *There's more...* section for more details.

We can force the `RidgeCV` object to store the cross-validation values; this will let us visualize what it's doing:

```
>>> alphas_to_test = np.linspace(0.01, 1)
>>> rcv3 = RidgeCV(alphas=alphas_to_test, store_cv_values=True)
>>> rcv3.fit(reg_data, reg_target)
```

As you can see, we test a bunch of points (50 in total) between 0.01 and 1. Since we passed `store_cv_values` as `true`, we can access these values:

```
>>> rcv3.cv_values_.shape
(100, 50)
```

So, we had 100 values in the initial regression and tested 50 different alpha values. We now have access to the errors of all 50 values. So, we can now find the smallest mean error and choose it as alpha:

```
>>> smallest_idx = rcv3.cv_values_.mean(axis=0).argmin()
>>> alphas_to_test[smallest_idx]
```

The question that arises is *"Does RidgeCV agree with our choice?"* Use the following command to find out:

```
>>> rcv3.alpha_
0.01
```

Beautiful!

It's also worthwhile to visualize what's going on. In order to do that, we'll plot the mean for all 50 test alphas.

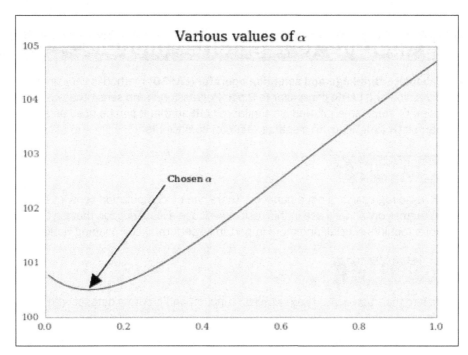

It's also worthwhile to visualize what's going on. In order to do that, we'll plot the mean for all 50 test alphas.

## There's more...

If we want to use our own scoring function, we can do that as well. Since we looked up MAD before, let's use it to score the differences. First, we need to define our loss function:

```
>>> def MAD(target, predictions):
        absolute_deviation = np.abs(target - predictions)
        return absolute_deviation.mean()
```

After we define the loss function, we can employ the `make_scorer` function in `sklearn`. This will take care of standardizing our function so that scikit's objects know how to use it. Also, because this is a loss function and not a score function, the lower the better, and thus the need to let `sklearn` to flip the sign to turn this from a maximization problem into a minimization problem:

```
>>> import sklearn
>>> MAD = sklearn.metrics.make_scorer(MAD, greater_is_better=False)
>>> rcv4 = RidgeCV(alphas=alphas_to_test, store_cv_values=True,
                   scoring=MAD)
>>> rcv4.fit(reg_data, reg_target)
```

```
>>> smallest_idx = rcv4.cv_values_.mean(axis=0).argmin()
>>> alphas_to_test[smallest_idx]
0.2322
```

# Using sparsity to regularize models

The **least absolute shrinkage and selection operator** (**LASSO**) method is very similar to ridge regression and LARS. It's similar to Ridge Regression in the sense that we penalize our regression by some amount, and it's similar to LARS in that it can be used as a parameter selection, and it typically leads to a sparse vector of coefficients.

## Getting ready

To be clear, lasso regression is not a panacea. There can be computation consequences to using lasso regression. As we'll see in this recipe, we'll use a loss function that isn't differential, and therefore, requires special, and more importantly, performance-impairing workarounds.

## How to do it...

Let's go back to the trusty `make_regression` function and create a dataset with the same parameters:

```
>>> from sklearn.datasets import make_regression
>>> reg_data, reg_target = make_regression(n_samples=200, n_features=500,
                            n_informative=5, noise=5)
```

Next, we need to import the `Lasso` object:

```
>>> from sklearn.linear_model import Lasso
>>> lasso = Lasso()
```

Lasso contains many parameters, but the most interesting parameter is `alpha`. It scales the penalization term of the `Lasso` method, which we'll look at in the *How it works...* section. For now, leave it as `1`. As an aside, and much like ridge regression, if this term is `0`, lasso is equivalent to linear regression:

```
>>> lasso.fit(reg_data, reg_target)
```

Again, let's see how many of the coefficients remain nonzero:

```
>>> np.sum(lasso.coef_ != 0)
9

>>> lasso_0 = Lasso(0)
>>> lasso_0.fit(reg_data, reg_target)
```

```
>>> np.sum(lasso_0.coef_ != 0)
500
```

None of our coefficients turn out to be 0, which is what we expect. Actually, if you run this, you might get a warning from scikit-learn that advises you to choose `LinearRegression`.

## How it works...

For linear regression, we minimized the squared error. Here, we're still going to minimize the squared error, but we'll add a penalization term that will induce the scarcity. The equation looks like the following:

$$\sum e_i + \lambda \|\beta\|_1$$

An alternate way of looking at this is to minimize the residual sum of squares:

$$RSS(\beta) \text{ such that } \|\beta\|_1 < \beta$$

This constraint is what leads to the scarcity. Lasso regression's constraint creates a hypercube around the origin (the coefficients being the axis), which means that the most extreme points are the corners, where many of the coefficients are 0. Ridge regression creates a hypersphere due to the constraint of the l2 norm being less than some constant, but it's very likely that coefficients will not be zero even if they are constrained.

### Lasso cross-validation

Choosing the most appropriate lambda is a critical problem. We can specify the lambda ourselves or use cross-validation to find the best choice given the data at hand:

```
>>> from sklearn.linear_model import LassoCV
>>> lassocv = LassoCV()
>>> lassocv.fit(reg_data, reg_target)
```

`lassocv` will have, as an attribute, the most appropriate lambda. scikit-learn mostly uses alpha in its notation, but the literature uses lambda:

```
>>> lassocv.alpha_
0.80722126078646139
```

The number of coefficients can be accessed in the regular manner:

```
>>> lassocv.coef_[:5]
array([0., 42.41, 0.,0., -0.])
```

Letting `lassocv` choose the appropriate best fit leaves us with 11 nonzero coefficients:

```
>>> np.sum(lassocv.coef_ != 0)
11
```

## Lasso for feature selection

Lasso can often be used for feature selection for other methods. For example, you might run lasso regression to get the appropriate number of features, and then use these features in another algorithm.

To get the features we want, create a masking array based on the columns that aren't zero, and then filter to keep the features we want:

```
>>> mask = lassocv.coef_ != 0
>>> new_reg_data = reg_data[:, mask]
>>> new_reg_data.shape
(200, 11)
```

# Taking a more fundamental approach to regularization with LARS

To borrow from Gilbert Strang's evaluation of the Gaussian elimination, LARS is an idea you probably would've considered eventually had it not been discovered previously by Efron, Hastie, Johnstone, and Tibshiriani in their works[1].

## Getting ready

Least-angle regression (LARS) is a regression technique that is well suited for high-dimensional problems, that is, $p \gg n$, where $p$ denotes the columns or features and $n$ is the number of samples.

## How to do it...

First, import the necessary objects. The data we use will have 200 data points and 500 features. We'll also choose a low noise and a small number of informative features:

```
>>> from sklearn.datasets import make_regression
>>> reg_data, reg_target = make_regression(n_samples=200,
                      n_features=500, n_informative=10, noise=2)
```

Since we used 10 informative features, let's also specify that we want 10 nonzero coefficients in LARS. We will probably not know the exact number of informative features beforehand, but it's useful for learning purposes:

```
>>> from sklearn.linear_model import Lars
>>> lars = Lars(n_nonzero_coefs=10)
>>> lars.fit(reg_data, reg_target)
```

We can then verify that LARS returns the correct number of nonzero coefficients:

```
>>> np.sum(lars.coef_ != 0)
10
```

The question then is why it is more useful to use a smaller number of features. To illustrate this, let's hold out half of the data and train two LARS models, one with 12 nonzero coefficients and another with no predetermined amount. We use 12 here because we might have an idea of the number of important features, but we might not be sure of the exact number:

```
>>> train_n = 100
>>> lars_12 = Lars(n_nonzero_coefs=12)
>>> lars_12.fit(reg_data[:train_n], reg_target[:train_n])

>>> lars_500 = Lars() # it's 500 by default
>>> lars_500.fit(reg_data[:train_n], reg_target[:train_n]);
```

Now, to see how well each feature fit the unknown data, do the following:

```
>>> np.mean(np.power(reg_target[train_n:] - lars_12.predict(reg_data
            [train_n:]), 2))
31.527714163321001
>>> np.mean(np.power(reg_target[train_n:] - lars_500.predict(reg_data
            [train_n:]), 2))
9.6198147535136237e+30
```

Look again if you missed it; the error on the test set was clearly very high. Herein lies the problem with high-dimensional datasets; given a large number of features, it's typically not too difficult to get a model of good fit on the train sample, but overfitting becomes a huge problem.

## How it works...

LARS works by iteratively choosing features that are correlated with the residuals. Geometrically, correlation is effectively the least angle between the feature and the residuals; this is how LARS gets its name.

After choosing the first feature, LARS will continue to move in the least angle direction, until a different feature has the same amount of correlation with the residuals. Then, LARS will begin to move in the combined direction of both features. To visualize this, consider the following graph:

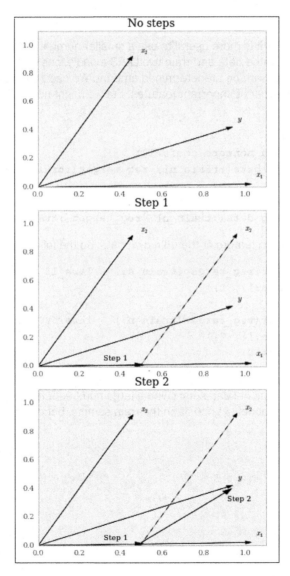

So, we move along **x1** until we get to the point where the *pull* on **x1** by **y** is the same as the *pull* on **x2** by **y**. When this occurs, we move along the path that is equal to the angle between **x1** and **x2** divided by 2.

## There's more...

Much in the same way we used cross-validation to tune ridge regression, we can do the same with LARS:

```
>>> from sklearn.linear_model import LarsCV
>>> lcv = LarsCV()
>>> lcv.fit(reg_data, reg_target)
```

Using cross-validation will help us determine the best number of nonzero coefficients to use. Here, it turns out to be as shown:

```
>>> np.sum(lcv.coef_ != 0)
44
```

[1]: Efron, Bradley; Hastie, Trevor; Johnstone, Iain and Tibshirani, Robert (2004). "Least Angle Regression". Annals of Statistics 32(2): pp. 407–499. doi:10.1214/009053604000000067. MR 2060166.

# Using linear methods for classification – logistic regression

Linear models can actually be used for classification tasks. This involves fitting a linear model to the probability of a certain class, and then using a function to create a threshold at which we specify the outcome of one of the classes.

## Getting ready

The function used here is typically the logistic function (surprise!). It's a pretty simple function:

$$f(x) = \frac{1}{1 + e^{-t}}$$

Visually, it looks like the following:

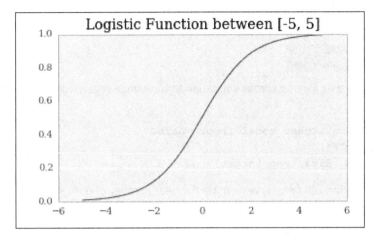

Let's use the `make_classification` method, create a dataset, and get to classifying:

```
>>> from sklearn.datasets import make_classification
>>> X, y = make_classification(n_samples=1000, n_features=4)
```

## How to do it...

The `LogisticRegression` object works in the same way as the other linear models:

```
>>> from sklearn.linear_model import LogisticRegression
>>> lr = LogisticRegression()
```

Since we're good data scientists, we will pull out the last 200 samples to test the trained model on. Since this is a random dataset, it's fine to hold out the last 200; if you're dealing with structured data, don't do this (for example, if you deal with time series data):

```
>>> X_train = X[:-200]
>>> X_test = X[-200:]
>>> y_train = y[:-200]
>>> y_test = y[-200:]
```

We'll discuss more on cross-validation later in the book. Now, we need to fit the model with logistic regression. We'll keep around the predictions on the train set, just like the test set. It's a good idea to see how often you are correct on both sets. Often, you'll be better on the train set; it's a matter of how much worse you are on the test set:

```
>>> lr.fit(X_train, y_train)
>>> y_train_predictions = lr.predict(X_train)
>>> y_test_predictions = lr.predict(X_test)
```

Now that we have the predictions, let's take a look at how good our predictions were. Here, we'll simply look at the number of times we were correct; later, we'll talk about evaluating classification models in more detail.

The calculation is simple; it's the number of times we were correct over the total sample:

```
>>> (y_train_predictions == y_train).sum().astype(float) /
                   y_train.shape[0]
0.8662499
```

And now the test sample:

```
>>> (y_test_predictions == y_test).sum().astype(float) /
                   y_test.shape[0]
0.900000
```

So, here we were correct about as often in the test set as we were in the train set. Sadly, in practice, this isn't often the case.

The question then changes to how to move on from the logistic function to a method by which we can classify groups.

First, recall the linear regression hopes offending the linear function that fits the expected value of *Y*, given the values of *X*; this is $E(Y|X) = X\beta$. Here, the *Y* values are the probabilities of the classes. Therefore, the problem we're trying to solve is $E(p|X) = \backslash X\beta$. Then, once the threshold is applied, this becomes *Logit(p) = Xβ*. The idea expanded is how other forms of regression work, for example, Poisson.

## There's more...

You'll surely see this again. There will be a situation where one class is weighted differently from the other classes; for example, one class may be 99 percent of cases. This situation will pop up all over the place in the classification work. The canonical example is fraud detection, where most transactions aren't fraud, but the cost associated with misclassification is asymmetric between classes.

Let's create a classification problem with 95 percent imbalance and see how the basic stock logistic regression handles this case:

```
>>> X, y = make_classification(n_samples=5000, n_features=4,
        weights=[.95])

>>> sum(y) / (len(y)*1.) #to confirm the class imbalance
0.0555
```

Create the train and test sets, and then fit logistic regression:

```
>>> X_train = X[:-500]
>>> X_test = X[-500:]
>>> y_train = y[:-500]
>>> y_test = y[-500:]

>>> lr.fit(X_train, y_train)
>>> y_train_predictions = lr.predict(X_train)
>>> y_test_predictions = lr.predict(X_test)
```

Now, to see how well our model fits the data, do the following:

```
>>> (y_train_predictions == y_train).sum().astype(float) /
    y_train.shape[0]
>>> 0.96977
```

```
>>> (y_test_predictions == y_test).sum().astype(float) / y_test.shape[0]
>>> 0.97999
```

At first, it looks like we did well, but it turns out that when we always guessed that a transaction was not fraud (or class 0 in general) we were right around 95 percent of the time. If we look at how well we did in classifying the 1 class, it's not nearly as good:

```
>>> (y_test[y_test==1] == y_test_predictions[y_test==1])
    .sum().astype(float) / y_test[y_test==1].shape[0]
0.583333
```

Hypothetically, we might care more about identifying fraud cases than non-fraud cases; this could be due to a business rule, so we might alter how we weigh the correct and incorrect values.

By default, the classes are weighted (and thus resampled) in accordance with the inverse of the class weights of the training set. However, because we care more about fraud cases, let's oversample the fraud relative to nonfraud cases.

We know that our relative weighting right now is 95 percent nonfraud; let's change this to overweight fraud cases:

```
>>> lr = LogisticRegression(class_weight={0: .15, 1: .85})
>>> lr.fit(X_train, y_train)
```

Let's predict the outputs again:

```
>>> y_train_predictions = lr.predict(X_train)
>>> y_test_predictions = lr.predict(X_test)
```

We can see that we did a much better job on classifying the fraud cases:

```
>>> (y_test[y_test==1] == y_test_predictions[y_test==1]).sum().
astype(float) / y_test[y_test==1].shape[0]
0.875
```

But, at what expense do we do this? To find out, use the following command:

```
>>> (y_test_predictions == y_test).sum().astype(float) / y_test.shape[0]
0.967999
```

Here, there's only about 1 percent less accuracy. Whether that's okay depends on your problem. Put in the context of the problem, if the estimated cost associated with fraud is sufficiently large, it can eclipse the cost associated with tracking fraud.

# Directly applying Bayesian ridge regression

In the *Using ridge regression to overcome linear regression's shortfalls* recipe, we discussed the connections between the constraints imposed by ridge regression from an optimization standpoint. We also discussed the Bayesian interpretation of priors on the coefficients, which attract the mass of the density towards the prior, which often has a mean of 0.

So, now we'll look at how we can directly apply this interpretation though scikit-learn.

## Getting ready

Ridge and lasso regression can both be understood through a Bayesian lens as opposed to an optimization lens. Only Bayesian ridge regression is implemented by scikit-learn, but in the *How it works...* section, we'll look at both cases.

First, as usual, let's create some regression data:

```
>>> from sklearn.datasets import make_regression
>>> X, y = make_regression(1000, 10, n_informative=2, noise=20)
```

## How to do it...

We can just "throw" ridge regression at the problem with a few simple steps:

```
>>> from sklearn.linear_model import BayesianRidge

>>> br = BayesianRidge()
```

The two sets of coefficients of interest are `alpha_1/alpha_2` and `lambda_1/lambda_2`. The alphas are the hyperparameters for the prior over the alpha parameter, and the lambda are the hyperparameters of the prior over the lambda parameter.

First, let's fit a model without any modification to the hyperparameters:

```
>>> br.fit(X, y)
>>> br.coef_
array([ 0.3000136 , -0.33023408, 68.166673, -0.63228159, 0.07350987,
        -0.90736606, 0.38851709, -0.8085291 , 0.97259451, 68.73538646])
```

Now, if we modify the hyperparameters, notice the slight changes in the coefficients:

```
>>> br_alphas = BayesianRidge(alpha_1=10, lambda_1=10)
>>> br_alphas.fit(X, y)
>>> br_alphas.coef_
array([ 0.30054387, -0.33130025, 68.10432626, -0.63056712,
        0.07751436, -0.90919326, 0.39020878, -0.80822013,
        0.97497567, 68.67409658])
```

## How it works...

For Bayesian ridge regression, we assume a prior over the errors and alpha. Both these priors are gamma distributions.

The gamma distribution is a very flexible distribution. Here are some of the different shapes the gamma distribution can take given the different parameterization techniques for location and scale. **1e-06** is the default parameterization of `BayesianRidge` in scikit-learn:

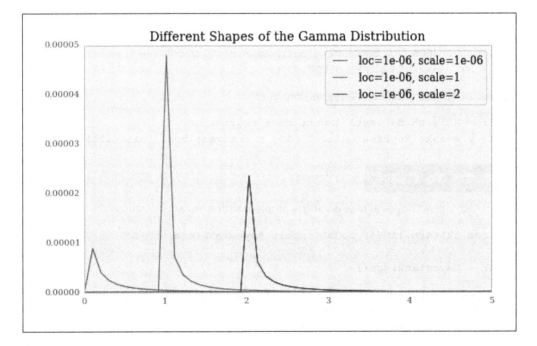

As you can see, the coefficients are naturally shrunk towards 0, especially with a very small location parameter.

## There's more...

Like I mentioned earlier, there's also a Bayesian interpretation of lasso regression. Imagine we set priors over the coefficients; remember that they are random numbers themselves. For lasso regression, we will choose a prior that naturally produces 0s, for example, the double exponential.

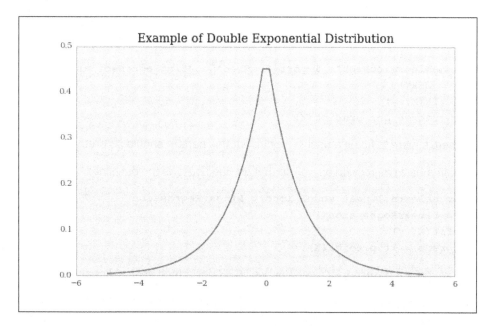

Notice the peak around **0**. This will naturally lead to the zero coefficients in lasso regression. By tuning the hyperparameters, it's also possible to create 0 coefficients that more or less depend on the setup of the problem.

# Using boosting to learn from errors

Gradient boosting regression is a technique that learns from its mistakes. Essentially, it tries to fit a bunch of weak learners. There are two things to note:

- Individually, each learner has poor accuracy, but together they can have very good accuracy
- They're applied sequentially, which means that each learner becomes an expert in the mistakes of the prior learner

## Getting ready

Let's use some basic regression data and see how **gradient boosting** regression (henceforth, GBR) works:

```
>>> from sklearn.datasets import make_regression
>>> X, y = make_regression(1000, 2, noise=10)
```

## How to do it...

GBR is part of the ensemble module because it's an ensemble learner. This is the name for the idea behind using many weak learners to simulate a strong learner:

```
>>> from sklearn.ensemble import GradientBoostingRegressor as GBR
>>> gbr = GBR()
>>> gbr.fit(X, y)
>>> gbr_preds = gbr.predict(X)
```

Clearly, there's more to fitting a usable model, but this pattern should be pretty clear by now.

Now, let's fit a basic regression as well so that we can use it as the baseline:

```
>>> from sklearn.linear_model import LinearRegression
>>> lr = LinearRegression()
>>> lr.fit(X, y)
>>> lr_preds = lr.predict(X)
```

Now that we have a baseline, let's see how well GBR performed against linear regression.

I'll leave it as an exercise for you to plot the residuals, but to get started, do the following:

```
>>> gbr_residuals = y - gbr_preds
>>> lr_residuals = y - lr_preds
```

The following will be the output:

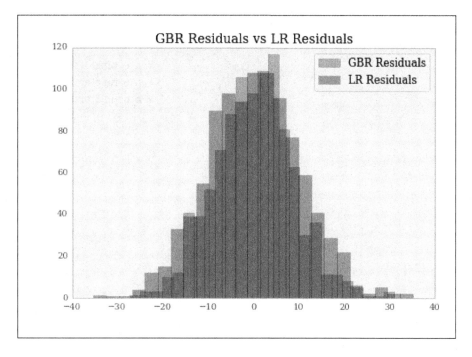

It looks like GBR has a better fit, but it's a bit hard to tell. Let's take the 95 percent CI and compare:

```
>>> np.percentile(gbr_residuals, [2.5, 97.5])
array([-16.05443674,  17.53946294])

>>> np.percentile(lr_residuals, [2.5, 97.5])
array([-20.05434912,  19.80272884])
```

So, GBR clearly fits a bit better; we can also make several modifications to the GBR algorithm, which might improve performance. I'll show an example here, then we'll walkthrough the different options in the *How it works...* section:

```
>>> n_estimators = np.arange(100, 1100, 350)
>>> gbrs = [GBR(n_estimators=n_estimator) for n_estimator in
            n_estimators]
>>> residuals = {}
>>> for i, gbr in enumerate(gbrs):
        gbr.fit(X, y)
        residuals[gbr.n_estimators] = y - gbr.predict(X)
```

The following is the output:

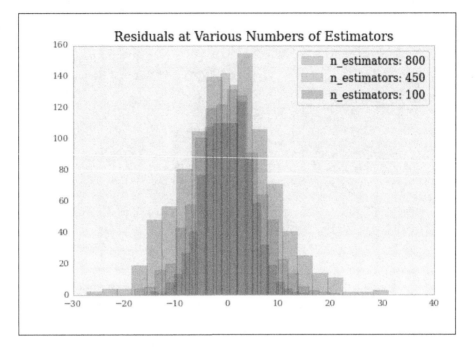

It's a bit muddled, but hopefully, it's clear that as the number of estimators increases, the error goes down. Sadly, this isn't a panacea; first, we don't test against a holdout set, and second, as the number of estimators goes up, the training time takes longer. This isn't a big deal on the dataset we use here, but imagine one or two magnitudes higher.

## How it works...

The first parameter, and the one we already looked at, is n_estimators—the number of weak learners that are used in GBR. In general, if you can get away with more (that is, have enough computational power), it is probably better. There are more nuances to the other parameters.

You should tune the max_depth parameter before all others. Since the individual learners are trees, max_depth controls how many nodes are produced for the trees. There's a subtle line between using the appropriate number of nodes that can fit the data well and using too many, which might cause overfitting.

The loss parameter controls the loss function, which determines the error. The ls parameter is the default, and stands for least squares. Least absolute deviation, Huber loss, and quantiles are also available.

# 3
# Building Models with Distance Metrics

This chapter will cover the following topics:

- ▶ Using KMeans to cluster data
- ▶ Optimizing the number of centroids
- ▶ Assessing cluster correctness
- ▶ Using MiniBatch KMeans to handle more data
- ▶ Quantizing an image with KMeans clustering
- ▶ Finding the closest objects in the feature space
- ▶ Probabilistic clustering with Gaussian Mixture Models
- ▶ Using KMeans for outlier detection
- ▶ Using k-NN for regression

## Introduction

In this chapter, we'll cover clustering. Clustering is often grouped together with unsupervised techniques. These techniques assume that we do not know the outcome variable. This leads to ambiguity in outcomes and objectives in practice, but nevertheless, clustering can be useful. As we'll see, we can use clustering to "localize" our estimates in a supervised setting. This is perhaps why clustering is so effective; it can handle a wide range of situations, and often, the results are for the lack of a better term, "sane".

We'll walk through a wide variety of applications in this chapter; from image processing to regression and outlier detection. Through these applications, we'll see that clustering can often be viewed through a probabilistic or optimization lens. Different interpretations lead to various trade-offs. We'll walk through how to fit the models here so that you have the tools to try out many models when faced with a clustering problem.

# Using KMeans to cluster data

Clustering is a very useful technique. Often, we need to divide and conquer when taking actions. Consider a list of potential customers for a business. A business might need to group customers into cohorts, and then departmentalize responsibilities for these cohorts. Clustering can help facilitate the clustering process.

KMeans is probably one of the most well-known clustering algorithms and, in a larger sense, one of the most well-known unsupervised learning techniques.

## Getting ready

First, let's walk through some simple clustering, then we'll talk about how KMeans works:

```
>>> from sklearn.datasets import make_blobs
>>> blobs, classes = make_blobs(500, centers=3)
```

Also, since we'll be doing some plotting, import `matplotlib` as shown:

```
>>> import matplotlib.pyplot as plt
```

## How to do it...

We are going to walk through a simple example that clusters blobs of fake data. Then we'll talk a little bit about how KMeans works to find the optimal number of blobs.

Looking at our blobs, we can see that there are three distinct clusters:

```
>>> f, ax = plt.subplots(figsize=(7.5, 7.5))
>>> ax.scatter(blobs[:, 0], blobs[:, 1], color=rgb[classes])
>>> rgb = np.array(['r', 'g', 'b'])
>>> ax.set_title("Blobs")
```

The output is as follows:

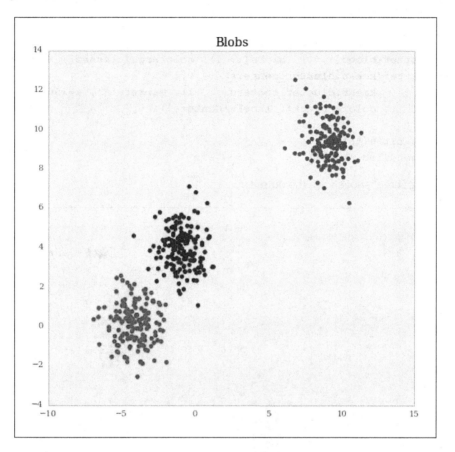

Now we can use KMeans to find the centers of these clusters. In the first example, we'll pretend we know that there are three centers:

```
>>> from sklearn.cluster import KMeans
>>> kmean = KMeans(n_clusters=3)
>>> kmean.fit(blobs)
KMeans(copy_x=True, init='k-means++', max_iter=300, n_clusters=3,
        n_init=10, n_jobs=1, precompute_distances=True,
        random_state=None, tol=0.0001, verbose=0)

>>> kmean.cluster_centers_
array([[ 0.47819567,  1.80819197],
```

```
[ 0.08627847,  8.24102715],
[ 5.2026125 ,  7.86881767]])

>>> f, ax = plt.subplots(figsize=(7.5, 7.5))
>>> ax.scatter(blobs[:, 0], blobs[:, 1], color=rgb[classes])
>>> ax.scatter(kmean.cluster_centers_[:, 0],
               kmean.cluster_centers_[:, 1], marker='*', s=250,
               color='black', label='Centers')

>>> ax.set_title("Blobs")
>>> ax.legend(loc='best')
```

The following screenshot shows the output:

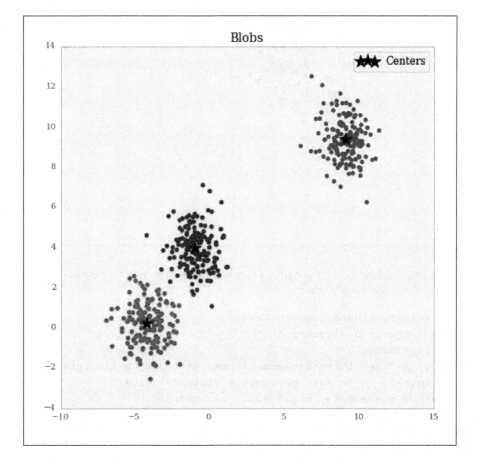

Other attributes are useful too. For instance, the `labels_` attribute will produce the expected label for each point:

```
>>> kmean.labels_[:5]
array([1, 1, 2, 2, 1], dtype=int32)
```

We can check whether `kmean.labels_` is the same as classes, but because KMeans has no knowledge of the classes going in, it cannot assign the sample index values to both classes:

```
>>> classes[:5]
array([0, 0, 2, 2, 0])
```

Feel free to swap 1 and 0 in classes to see if it matches up with `labels_`.

The `transform` function is quite useful in the sense that it will output the distance between each point and centroid:

```
>>> kmean.transform(blobs)[:5]
array([[ 6.47297373,  1.39043536,  6.4936008 ],
       [ 6.78947843,  1.51914705,  3.67659072],
       [ 7.24414567,  5.42840092,  0.76940367],
       [ 8.56306214,  5.78156881,  0.89062961],
       [ 7.32149254,  0.89737788,  5.12246797]])
```

## How it works...

KMeans is actually a very simple algorithm that works to minimize the within-cluster sum of square distances from the mean. We'll be minimizing the sum of squares yet again!

It does this by first setting a pre-specified number of clusters, *K*, and then alternating between the following:

- ▶ Assigning each observation to the nearest cluster
- ▶ Updating each centroid by calculating the mean of each observation assigned to this cluster

This happens until some specified criterion is met.

# Optimizing the number of centroids

Centroids are difficult to interpret, and it can also be very difficult to determine whether we have the correct number of centroids. It's important to understand whether your data is unlabeled or not as this will directly influence the evaluation measures we can use.

## Getting ready

Evaluating the model performance for unsupervised techniques is a challenge. Consequently, `sklearn` has several methods to evaluate clustering when a ground truth is known, and very few for when it isn't.

We'll start with a single cluster model and evaluate its similarity. This is more for the purpose of mechanics as measuring the similarity of one cluster count is clearly not useful in finding the ground truth number of clusters.

## How to do it...

To get started we'll create several blobs that can be used to simulate clusters of data:

```
>>> from sklearn.datasets import make_blobs
>>> import numpy as np
>>> blobs, classes = make_blobs(500, centers=3)

>>> from sklearn.cluster import KMeans
>>> kmean = KMeans(n_clusters=3)
>>> kmean.fit(blobs)
KMeans(copy_x=True, init='k-means++', max_iter=300, n_clusters=3,
       n_init=10, n_jobs=1, precompute_distances=True,
       random_state=None, tol=0.0001, verbose=0)
```

First, we'll look at silhouette distance. **Silhouette distance** is the ratio of the difference between in-cluster dissimilarity, the closest out-of-cluster dissimilarity, and the maximum of these two values. It can be thought of as a measure of how separate the clusters are.

Let's look at the distribution of distances from the points to the cluster centers; it's useful to understand silhouette distances:

```
>>> from sklearn import metrics
>>> silhouette_samples = metrics.silhouette_samples(blobs,
                         kmean.labels_)
>>> np.column_stack((classes[:5], silhouette_samples[:5]))

array([[ 1.,    0.87617292],
       [ 1.,    0.89082363],
```

```
       [ 1.,   0.88544994],
       [ 1.,   0.91478369],
       [ 1.,   0.91308287]])
>>> f, ax = plt.subplots(figsize=(10, 5))

>>> ax.set_title("Hist of Silhouette Samples")
>>> ax.hist(silhouette_samples)
```

The following is the output:

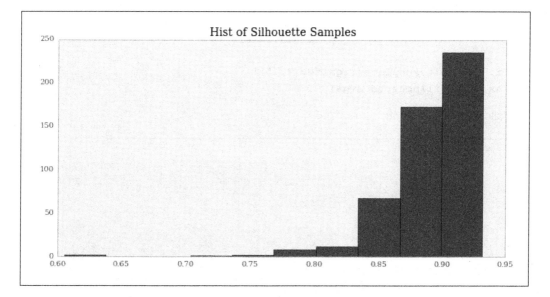

Notice that generally the higher the number of coefficients are closer to 1 (which is good) the better the score.

## How it works...

The average of the silhouette coefficients is often used to describe the entire model's fit:

```
>>> silhouette_samples.mean()
0.57130462953339578
```

It's very common; in fact, the metrics module exposes a function to arrive at the value we just got:

```
>>> metrics.silhouette_score(blobs, kmean.labels_)
0.57130462953339578
```

Now, let's fit the models of several cluster counts and see what the average silhouette score looks like:

```
# first new ground truth
>>> blobs, classes = make_blobs(500, centers=10)
>>> sillhouette_avgs = []

# this could take a while
>>> for k in range(2, 60):
        kmean = KMeans(n_clusters=k).fit(blobs)
        sillhouette_avgs.append(metrics.silhouette_score(blobs,
                             kmean.labels_))

>>> f, ax = plt.subplots(figsize=(7, 5))
>>> ax.plot(sillhouette_avgs)
```

The following is the output:

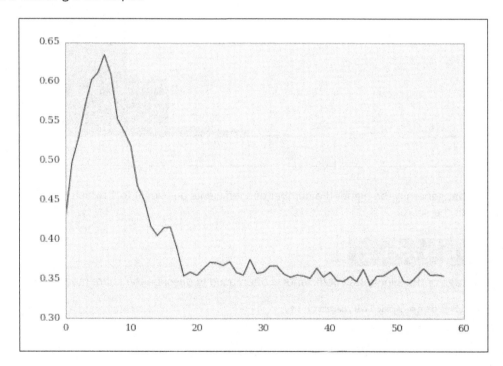

This plot shows that the silhouette averages as the number of centroids increase. We can see that the optimum number, according to the data generating process, is 3, but here it looks like it's around 6 or 7. This is the reality of clustering; quite often, we won't get the correct number of clusters, we can only really hope to estimate the number of clusters to some approximation.

# Assessing cluster correctness

We talked a little bit about assessing clusters when the ground truth is not known. However, we have not yet talked about assessing KMeans when the cluster is known. In a lot of cases, this isn't knowable; however, if there is outside annotation, we will know the ground truth, or at least the proxy, sometimes.

## Getting ready

So, let's assume a world where we have some outside agent supplying us with the ground truth.

We'll create a simple dataset, evaluate the measures of correctness against the ground truth in several ways, and then discuss them:

```
>>> from sklearn import datasets
>>> from sklearn import cluster
>>> blobs, ground_truth = datasets.make_blobs(1000, centers=3,
                                               cluster_std=1.75)
```

## How to do it...

Before we walk through the metrics, let's take a look at the dataset:

```
>>> f, ax = plt.subplots(figsize=(7, 5))

>>> colors = ['r', 'g', 'b']

>>> for i in range(3):
        p = blobs[ground_truth == i]
        ax.scatter(p[:,0], p[:,1], c=colors[i],
        label="Cluster {}".format(i))

>>> ax.set_title("Cluster With Ground Truth")
>>> ax.legend()

>>> f.savefig("9485OS_03-16")
```

The following is the output:

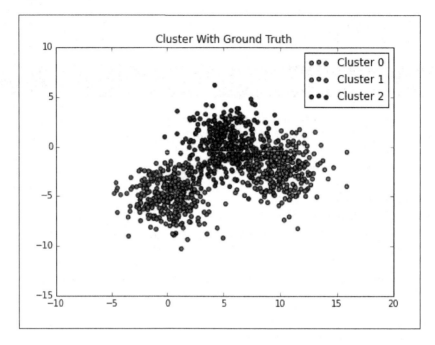

In order to fit a KMeans model we'll create a KMeans object from the `cluster` module:

```
>>> kmeans = cluster.KMeans(n_clusters=3)

>>> kmeans.fit(blobs)

KMeans(copy_x=True, init='k-means++', max_iter=300, n_clusters=3,
       n_init=10, n_jobs=1, precompute_distances=True,
       random_state=None, tol=0.0001, verbose=0)

>>> kmeans.cluster_centers_

array([[  5.18993766,   0.35110059],
       [  0.18300097,  -4.9480336 ],
       [ 10.01421381,  -2.26274328]])
```

Now that we've fit the model, let's have a look at the cluster centroids:

```
>>> f, ax = plt.subplots(figsize=(7, 5))

>>> colors = ['r', 'g', 'b']

>>> for i in range(3):
```

```
        p = blobs[ground_truth == i]
        ax.scatter(p[:,0], p[:,1], c=colors[i],
        label="Cluster {}".format(i))

>>> ax.scatter(kmeans.cluster_centers_[:, 0],
            kmeans.cluster_centers_[:, 1], s=100, color='black',
            label='Centers')
>>> ax.set_title("Cluster With Ground Truth")
>>> ax.legend()

>>> f.savefig("94850S_03-17")
```

The following is the output:

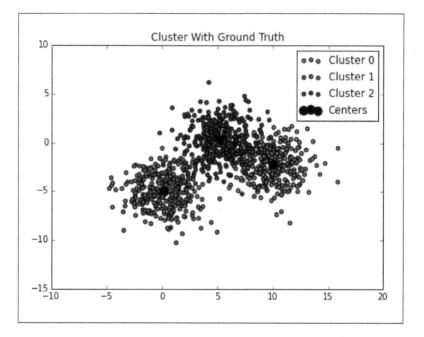

Now that we can view the clustering performance as a classification exercise, the metrics that are useful in its context are also useful here:

```
>>> for i in range(3):
        print (kmeans.labels_ == ground_truth)[ground_truth == i]
                .astype(int).mean()

0.0778443113772
0.990990990991
0.0570570570571
```

Clearly, we have some backward clusters. So, let's get this straightened out first, and then we'll look at the accuracy:

```
>>> new_ground_truth = ground_truth.copy()

>>> new_ground_truth[ground_truth == 0] = 2
>>> new_ground_truth[ground_truth == 2] = 0

>>> for i in range(3):
        print (kmeans.labels_ == new_ground_truth)[ground_truth == i]
                     .astype(int).mean()

0.919161676647
0.990990990991
0.90990990991
```

So, we're roughly correct 90 percent of the time. The second measure of similarity we'll look at is the mutual information score:

```
>>> from sklearn import metrics

>>> metrics.normalized_mutual_info_score(ground_truth, kmeans.labels_)

0.78533737204433651
```

As the score tends to be 0, the label assignments are probably not generated through similar processes; however, the score being closer to 1 means that there is a large amount of agreement between the two labels.

For example, let's look at what happens when the mutual information score itself:

```
>>> metrics.normalized_mutual_info_score(ground_truth, ground_truth)

1.0
```

Given the name, we can tell that there is probably an unnormalized `mutual_info_score`:

```
>>> metrics.mutual_info_score(ground_truth, kmeans.labels_)

0.78945287371677486
```

These are very close; however, normalized mutual information is the mutual information divided by the root of the product of the entropy of each set truth and assigned label.

## There's more...

One cluster metric we haven't talked about yet and one that is not reliant on the ground truth is inertia. It is not very well documented as a metric at the moment. However, it is the metric that KMeans minimizes.

**Inertia** is the sum of the squared difference between each point and its assigned cluster. We can use a little NumPy to determine this:

```
>>> kmeans.inertia_
```

# Using MiniBatch KMeans to handle more data

KMeans is a nice method to use; however, it is not ideal for a lot of data. This is due to the complexity of KMeans. This said, we can get approximate solutions with much better algorithmic complexity using KMeans.

## Getting ready

MiniBatch KMeans is a faster implementation of KMeans. KMeans is computationally very expensive; the problem is **NP-hard**.

However, using MiniBatch KMeans, we can speed up KMeans by orders of magnitude. This is achieved by taking many subsamples that are called MiniBatches. Given the convergence properties of subsampling, a close approximation to regular KMeans is achieved, given good initial conditions.

## How to do it...

Let's do some very high-level profiling of MiniBatch clustering. First, we'll look at the overall speed difference, and then we'll look at the errors in the estimates:

```
>>> from sklearn.datasets import make_blobs
>>> blobs, labels = make_blobs(int(1e6), 3)

>>> from sklearn.cluster import KMeans, MiniBatchKMeans

>>> kmeans = KMeans(n_clusters=3)
>>> minibatch = MiniBatchKMeans(n_clusters=3)
```

Understand that these metrics are meant to expose the issue. Therefore, great care is taken to ensure the highest accuracy of the benchmarks. There is a lot of information available on this topic; if you really want to get to the heart of why MiniBatch KMeans is better at scaling, it will be a good idea to review what's available.

Now that the setup is complete, we can measure the time difference:

```
>>> %time kmeans.fit(blobs) #IPython Magic
CPU times: user 8.17 s, sys: 881 ms, total: 9.05 s Wall time: 9.97 s

>>> %time minibatch.fit(blobs)
CPU times: user 4.04 s, sys: 90.1 ms, total: 4.13 s Wall time: 4.69 s
```

There's a large difference in CPU times. The difference in clustering performance is shown as follows:

```
>>> kmeans.cluster_centers_[0]
array([ 1.10522173, -5.59610761, -8.35565134])

>>> minibatch.cluster_centers_[0]
array([ 1.12071187, -5.61215116, -8.32015587])
```

The next question we might ask is how far apart the centers are:

```
>>> from sklearn.metrics import pairwise
>>> pairwise.pairwise_distances(kmeans.cluster_centers_[0],
                                minibatch.cluster_centers_[0])

array([[ 0.03305309]])
```

This seems to be very close. The diagonals will contain the cluster center differences:

```
>>> np.diag(pairwise.pairwise_distances(kmeans.cluster_centers_,
            minibatch.cluster_centers_))
array([ 0.04191979,  0.03133651,  0.04342707])
```

## How it works...

The batches here are key. Batches are iterated through to find the batch mean; for the next iteration, the prior batch mean is updated in relation to the current iteration. There are several options that dictate the general KMeans' behavior and parameters that determine how MiniBatch KMeans gets updated.

The `batch_size` parameter determines how large the batches should be. Just for fun, let's run MiniBatch; however, this time we set the batch size same as the dataset size:

```
>>> minibatch = MiniBatchKMeans(batch_size=len(blobs))
>>> %time minibatch.fit(blobs)
CPU times: user 34.6 s, sys: 3.17 s, total: 37.8 s Wall time: 44.6 s
```

Clearly, this is against the spirit of the problem, but it does illustrate an important point. Choosing poor initial conditions can affect how well models, particularly clustering models, converge. With MiniBatch KMeans, there is no guarantee that the global optimum will be achieved.

# Quantizing an image with KMeans clustering

Image processing is an important topic in which clustering has some application. It's worth pointing out that there are several very good image-processing libraries in Python. **scikit-image** is a "sister" project of scikit-learn. It's worth taking a look at if you want to do anything complicated.

## Getting ready

We will have some fun in this recipe. The goal is to use cluster to blur an image.

First, we'll make use of SciPy to read the image. The image is translated in a 3-dimensional array; the *x* and *y* coordinates describe the height and width, and the third dimension represents the RGB values for each image:

```
# in your terminal
$ wget http://blog.trenthauck.com/assets/headshot.jpg
```

## How do it...

Now, let's read the image in Python:

```
>>> from scipy import ndimage
>>> img = ndimage.imread("headshot.jpg")
>>> plt.imshow(img)
```

The following image is seen:

Hey, that's (a younger) me!

Now that we have the image, let's check its dimensions:

```
>>> img.shape
(420, 420, 3)
```

To actually quantize the image, we need to convert it into a two-dimensional array, with the length being 420 x 420 and the width being the RGB values. A better way to think about this is to have a bunch of data points in three-dimensional space and cluster the points to reduce the number of distant colors in the image—a simple way to put quantization.

First, let's reshape our array; it is a NumPy array, and thus trivial to work with:

```
>>> x, y, z = img.shape
>>> long_img = img.reshape(x*y, z)
>>> long_img.shape
(176400, 3)
```

Now we can start the clustering process. First, let's import the cluster module and create a KMeans object. We'll pass n_clusters=5 so that we have five clusters, or really, five distinct colors.

This will be a good recipe to practice using silhouette distance that we reviewed in the *Optimizing the number of centroids* recipe:

```
>>> from sklearn import cluster
>>> k_means = cluster.KMeans(n_clusters=5)
>>> k_means.fit(long_img)
```

Now that we have our fit KMeans objects, let's take a look at our colors:

```
>>> centers = k_means.cluster_centers_
>>> centers
array([[ 142.58775848,  206.12712986,  226.04416873],
       [  86.29356543,   68.86312505,   54.04770507],
       [ 194.36182899,  172.19845258,  149.65603813],
       [  24.67768412,   20.45778933,   16.19698314],
       [ 149.27801776,  132.19850659,  115.32729167]])
```

## How it works...

Now that we have the centers, the next thing we need is the labels. This will tell us which points should be associated with which clusters:

```
>>> labels = k_means.labels_
>>> labels[:5]
array([1, 1, 1, 1, 1], dtype=int32)
```

At this point, we require the simplest of NumPy array manipulation followed by a bit of reshaping, and we'll have the new image:

```
>>> plt.imshow(centers[labels].reshape(x, y, z))
```

The following is the resultant image:

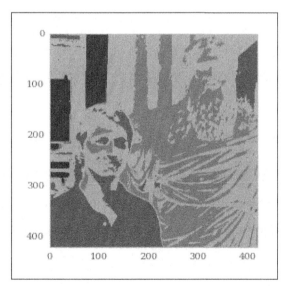

# Finding the closest objects in the feature space

Sometimes, the easiest thing to do is to just find the distance between two objects. We just need to find some distance metric, compute the pairwise distances, and compare the outcomes to what's expected.

## Getting ready

A lower-level utility in scikit-learn is `sklearn.metrics.pairwise`. This contains server functions to compute the distances between the vectors in a matrix X or the distances between the vectors in *X* and *Y* easily.

This can be useful for information retrieval. For example, given a set of customers with attributes of X, we might want to take a reference customer and find the closest customers to this customer. In fact, we might want to rank customers by the notion of similarity measured by a distance function. The quality of the similarity depends upon the feature space selection as well as any transformation we might do on the space.

We'll walk through several different scenarios of measuring distance.

## How to do it...

We will use the `pairwise_distances` function to determine the "closeness" of objects. Remember that the closeness is really just similarity that we use our distance function to grade.

First, let's import the pairwise distance function from the `metrics` module and create a dataset to play with:

```
>>> from sklearn.metrics import pairwise
>>> from sklearn.datasets import make_blobs
>>> points, labels = make_blobs()
```

This simplest way to check the distances is `pairwise_distances`:

```
>>> distances = pairwise.pairwise_distances(points)
```

`distances` is an *N* x *N* matrix with 0s along the diagonals. In the simplest case, let's see the distances between each point and the first point:

```
>>> np.diag(distances) [:5]
array([ 0.,   0.,   0.,   0.,   0.])
```

Now we can look for points that are closest to the first point in `points`:

```
>>> distances[0][:5]
array([  0., 11.82643041,1.23751545, 1.17612135, 14.61927874])
```

Ranking the points by closeness is very easy with `np.argsort`:

```
>>> ranks = np.argsort(distances[0])
>>> ranks[:5]
array([ 0, 27, 98, 23, 67])
```

The great thing about `argsort` is that now we can sort our `points` matrix to get the actual points:

```
>>> points[ranks][:5]
array([[ 8.96147382, -1.90405304],
       [ 8.75417014, -1.76289919],
       [ 8.78902665, -2.27859923],
       [ 8.59694131, -2.10057667],
       [ 8.70949958, -2.30040991]])
```

It's useful to see what the closest points look like. Other than some assurances, this works as intended:

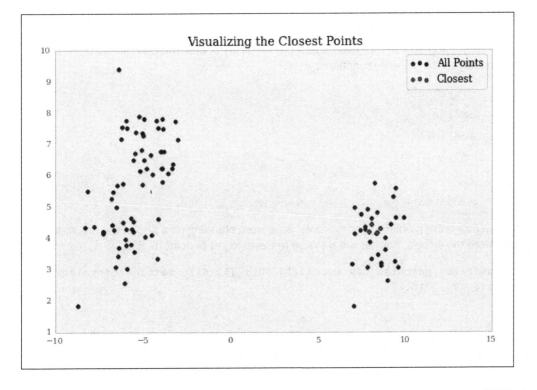

## How it works...

Given some distance function, each point is measured in a pairwise function. The default is the Euclidian distance, which is as follows:

$$d(x, y) = \sqrt{\sum_i (x_i - y_i)^2}$$

Verbally, this takes the difference between each component of the two vectors, squares the difference, sums them, and then takes the square root. This looks very familiar as we used something very similar to this when looking at the mean-squared error. If we take the square root, we have the same thing. In fact, a metric used often is **root-mean-square deviation** (**RMSE**), which is just the applied distance function.

In Python, this looks like the following:

```
>>> def euclid_distances(x, y):
        return np.power(np.power(x - y, 2).sum(), .5)
>>> euclid_distances(points[0], points[1])
11.826430406213145
```

There are several other functions available in scikit-learn, but scikit-learn will also use distance functions of SciPy. At the time of writing this book, the scikit-learn distance functions support sparse matrixes. Check out the SciPy documentation for more information on the distance functions:

- cityblock
- cosine
- euclidean
- l1
- l2
- manhattan

We can now solve problems. For example, if we were standing on a grid at the origin, and the lines were the streets, how far will we have to travel to get to point (5, 5)?.

```
>>> pairwise.pairwise_distances([[0, 0], [5, 5]], metric='cityblock')[0]
array([ 0.,  10.])
```

## There's more...

Using pairwise distances, we can find the similarity between bit vectors. It's a matter of finding the hamming distance, which is defined as follows:

$$\sum_i I_{x_i \neq y_i}$$

Use the following command:

```
>>> X = np.random.binomial(1, .5, size=(2, 4)).astype(np.bool)
>>> X
array([[False,  True, False, False],
       [False, False, False,  True]], dtype=bool)

>>> pairwise.pairwise_distances(X, metric='hamming')
array([[ 0. ,  0.25],
       [ 0.25,  0. ]])
```

# Probabilistic clustering with Gaussian Mixture Models

In KMeans, we assume that the variance of the clusters is equal. This leads to a subdivision of space that determines how the clusters are assigned; but, what about a situation where the variances are not equal and each cluster point has some probabilistic association with it?

## Getting ready

There's a more probabilistic way of looking at KMeans clustering. Hard KMeans clustering is the same as applying a Gaussian Mixture Model with a covariance matrix, S, which can be factored to the error times of the identity matrix. This is the same covariance structure for each cluster. It leads to **spherical clusters**.

However, if we allow S to vary, a GMM can be estimated and used for prediction. We'll look at how this works in a univariate sense, and then expand to more dimensions.

## How to do it...

First, we need to create some data. For example, let's simulate heights of both women and men. We'll use this example throughout this recipe. It's a simple example, but hopefully, will illustrate what we're trying to accomplish in an *N* dimensional space, which is a little easier to visualize:

```
>>> import numpy as np
>>> N = 1000

>>> in_m = 72
>>> in_w = 66

>>> s_m = 2
>>> s_w = s_m

>>> m = np.random.normal(in_m, s_m, N)
>>> w = np.random.normal(in_w, s_w, N)
>>> from matplotlib import pyplot as plt
>>> f, ax = plt.subplots(figsize=(7, 5))

>>> ax.set_title("Histogram of Heights")
>>> ax.hist(m, alpha=.5, label="Men");
>>> ax.hist(w, alpha=.5, label="Women");
>>> ax.legend()
```

The following is the output:

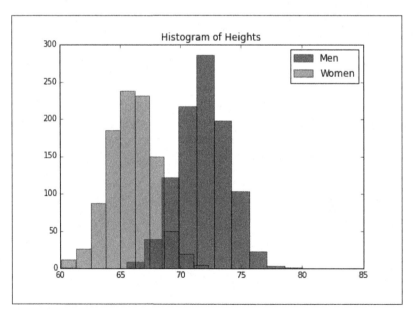

Next, we might be interested in subsampling the group, fitting the distribution, and then predicting the remaining groups:

```
>>> random_sample = np.random.choice([True, False], size=m.size)
>>> m_test = m[random_sample]
>>> m_train = m[~random_sample]

>>> w_test = w[random_sample]
>>> w_train = w[~random_sample]
```

Now we need to get the empirical distribution of the heights of both men and women based on the training set:

```
>>> from scipy import stats
>>> m_pdf = stats.norm(m_train.mean(), m_train.std())
>>> w_pdf = stats.norm(w_train.mean(), w_train.std())
```

For the test set, we will calculate based on the likelihood that the data point was generated from either distribution, and the most likely distribution will get the appropriate label assigned. We will, of course, look at how accurate we were:

```
>>> m_pdf.pdf(m[0])
0.043532673457165431

>>> w_pdf.pdf(m[0])
9.2341848872766183e-07
```

Notice the difference in likelihoods.

Assume that we guess situations when the men's probability is higher, but we overwrite them if the women's probability is higher:

```
>>> guesses_m = np.ones_like(m_test)
>>> guesses_m[m_pdf.pdf(m_test) < w_pdf.pdf(m_test)] = 0
```

Obviously, the question is how accurate we are. Since guesses_m will be 1 if we are correct, and 0 if we aren't, we take the mean of the vector and get the accuracy:

```
>>> guesses_m.mean()
0.93775100401606426
```

Not too bad! Now, to see how well we did with for the women's group, use the following commands:

```
>>> guesses_w = np.ones_like(w_test)
>>> guesses_w[m_pdf.pdf(w_test) > w_pdf.pdf(w_test)] = 0
>>> guesses_w.mean()
0.93172690763052213
```

Let's allow the variance to differ between groups. First, create some new data:

```
>>> s_m = 1
>>> s_w = 4

>>> m = np.random.normal(in_m, s_m, N)
>>> w = np.random.normal(in_w, s_w, N)
```

Then, create a training set:

```
>>> m_test = m[random_sample]
>>> m_train = m[~random_sample]

>>> w_test = w[random_sample]
>>> w_train = w[~random_sample]
>>> f, ax = plt.subplots(figsize=(7, 5))
>>> ax.set_title("Histogram of Heights")
>>> ax.hist(m_train, alpha=.5, label="Men");
>>> ax.hist(w_train, alpha=.5, label="Women");
>>> ax.legend()
```

Let's take a look at the difference in variances between the men and women:

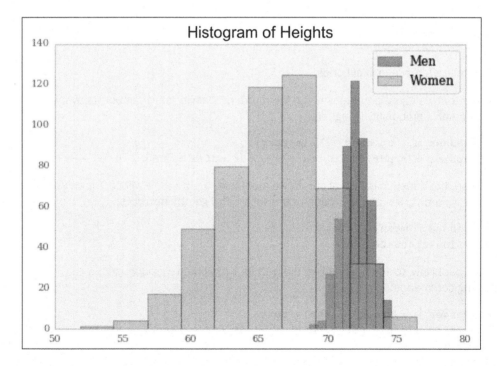

Now we can create the same PDFs:

```
>>> m_pdf = stats.norm(m_train.mean(), m_train.std())
>>> w_pdf = stats.norm(w_train.mean(), w_train.std())
```

The following is the output:

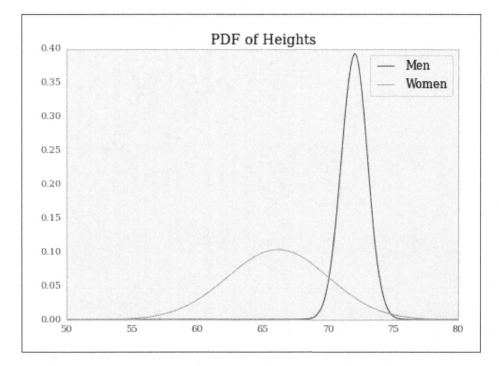

You can imagine this in a multidimensional space:

```
>>> class_A = np.random.normal(0, 1, size=(100, 2))
>>> class_B = np.random.normal(4, 1.5, size=(100, 2))
>>> f, ax = plt.subplots(figsize=(7, 5))

>>> ax.scatter(class_A[:,0], class_A[:,1], label='A', c='r')
>>> ax.scatter(class_B[:,0], class_B[:,1], label='B')
```

The following is the output:

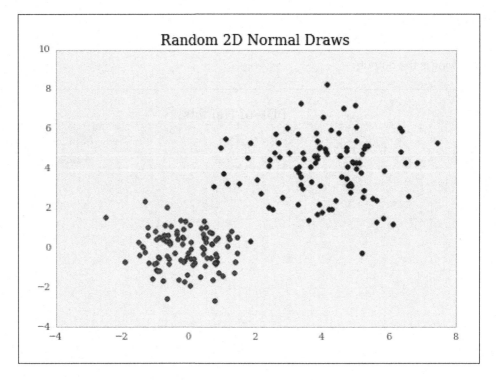

## How it works...

Okay, so now that we've looked at how we can classify points based on distribution, let's look at how we can do this in scikit-learn:

```
>>> from sklearn.mixture import GMM
>>> gmm = GMM(n_components=2)
>>> X = np.row_stack((class_A, class_B))
>>> y = np.hstack((np.ones(100), np.zeros(100)))
```

Since we're good little data scientists, we'll create a training set:

```
>>> train = np.random.choice([True, False], 200)
>>> gmm.fit(X[train])
GMM(covariance_type='diag', init_params='wmc', min_covar=0.001,
    n_components=2, n_init=1, n_iter=100, params='wmc',
    random_state=None,   thresh=0.01)
```

Fitting and predicting is done in the same way as fitting is done for many of the other objects in scikit-learn:

```
>>> gmm.fit(X[train])
>>> gmm.predict(X[train])[:5]
array([0, 0, 0, 0, 0])
```

There are other methods worth looking at now that the model has been fit.

For example, using `score_samples`, we can actually get the per-sample likelihood for each label.

# Using KMeans for outlier detection

In this chapter, we'll look at both the debate and mechanics of KMeans for outlier detection. It can be useful to isolate some types of errors, but care should be taken when using it.

## Getting ready

In this recipe, we'll use KMeans to do outlier detections on a cluster of points. It's important to note that there are many "camps" when it comes to outliers and outlier detection. On one hand, we're potentially removing points that were generated by the data-generating process by removing outliers. On the other hand, outliers can be due to a measurement error or some other outside factor.

This is the most credence we'll give to the debate; the rest of this recipe is about finding outliers; we'll work under the assumption that our choice to remove outliers is justified.

The act of outlier detection is a matter of finding the centroids of the clusters, and then identifying points that are potential outliers by their distances from the centroid.

## How to do it...

First, we'll generate a single blob of 100 points, and then we'll identify the 5 points that are furthest from the centroid. These are the potential outliers:

```
>>> from sklearn.datasets import make_blobs
>>> X, labels = make_blobs(100, centers=1)
>>> import numpy as np
```

It's important that the KMeans cluster has a single center. This idea is similar to a one-class SVM that is used for outlier detection:

```
>>> from sklearn.cluster import KMeans
>>> kmeans = KMeans(n_clusters=1)
>>> kmeans.fit(X)
```

Now, let's look at the plot. For those playing along at home, try to guess which points will be identified as one of the five outliers:

```
>>> f, ax = plt.subplots(figsize=(7, 5))
>>> ax.set_title("Blob")
>>> ax.scatter(X[:, 0], X[:, 1], label='Points')
>>> ax.scatter(kmeans.cluster_centers_[:, 0],
               kmeans.cluster_centers_[:, 1], label='Centroid',
               color='r')
>>> ax.legend()
```

The following is the output:

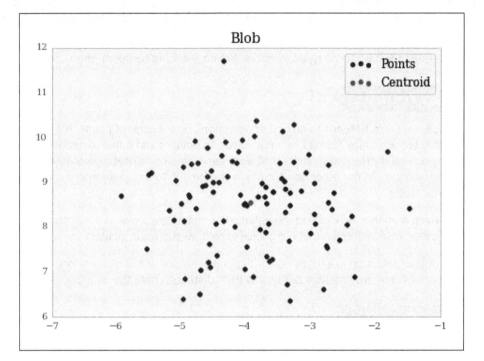

Now, let's identify the five closest points:

```
>>> distances = kmeans.transform(X)
# argsort returns an array of indexes which will sort the array in
ascending order
# so we reverse it via [::-1] and take the top five with [:5]
>>> sorted_idx = np.argsort(distances.ravel())[::-1][:5]
```

Now, let's see which plots are the farthest away:

```
>>> f, ax = plt.subplots(figsize=(7, 5))
>>> ax.set_title("Single Cluster")
>>> ax.scatter(X[:, 0], X[:, 1], label='Points')
>>> ax.scatter(kmeans.cluster_centers_[:, 0],
               kmeans.cluster_centers_[:, 1],
               label='Centroid', color='r')
>>> ax.scatter(X[sorted_idx][:, 0], X[sorted_idx][:, 1],
               label='Extreme Value', edgecolors='g',
               facecolors='none', s=100)
>>> ax.legend(loc='best')
```

The following is the output:

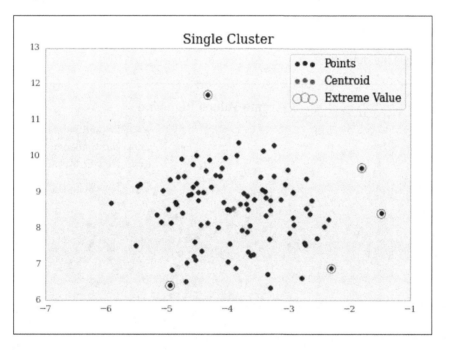

It's easy to remove these points if we like:

```
>>> new_X = np.delete(X, sorted_idx, axis=0)
```

Also, the centroid clearly changes with the removal of these points:

```
>>> new_kmeans = KMeans(n_clusters=1)
>>> new_kmeans.fit(new_X)
```

Let's visualize the difference between the old and new centroids:

```
>>> f, ax = plt.subplots(figsize=(7, 5))
>>> ax.set_title("Extreme Values Removed")
>>> ax.scatter(new_X[:, 0], new_X[:, 1], label='Pruned Points')
>>> ax.scatter(kmeans.cluster_centers_[:, 0],
               kmeans.cluster_centers_[:, 1], label='Old Centroid',
               color='r', s=80, alpha=.5)
>>> ax.scatter(new_kmeans.cluster_centers_[:, 0],
               new_kmeans.cluster_centers_[:, 1], label='New Centroid',
               color='m', s=80, alpha=.5)
>>> ax.legend(loc='best')
```

The following is the output:

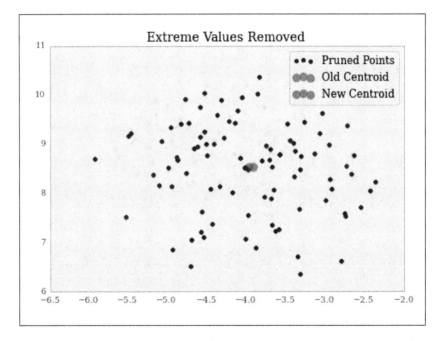

Clearly, the centroid hasn't moved much, which is to be expected when only removing the five most extreme values. This process can be repeated until we're satisfied that the data is representative of the process.

## How it works...

As we've already seen, there is a fundamental connection between the Gaussian distribution and the KMeans clustering. Let's create an empirical Gaussian based off the centroid and sample covariance matrix and look at the probability of each point—theoretically, the five points we removed. This just shows that we have in fact removed the values with the least likelihood. This idea between distances and likelihoods is very important, and will come around quite often in your machine learning training.

Use the following command to create an empirical Gaussian:

```
>>> from scipy import stats
>>> emp_dist = stats.multivariate_normal(
                kmeans.cluster_centers_.ravel())
>>> lowest_prob_idx = np.argsort(emp_dist.pdf(X))[:5]
>>> np.all(X[sorted_idx] == X[lowest_prob_idx])
True
```

# Using k-NN for regression

Regression is covered elsewhere in the book, but we might also want to run a regression on "pockets" of the feature space. We can think that our dataset is subject to several data processes. If this is true, only training on similar data points is a good idea.

## Getting ready

Our old friend, regression, can be used in the context of clustering. Regression is obviously a supervised technique, so we'll use **k-Nearest Neighbors** (**k-NN**) clustering rather than KMeans.

For the k-NN regression, we'll use the K closest points in the feature space to build the regression rather than using the entire space as in regular regression.

## How to do it...

For this recipe, we'll use the `iris` dataset. If we want to predict something such as the petal width for each flower, clustering by iris species can potentially give us better results. The k-NN regression won't cluster by the species, but we'll work under the assumption that the Xs will be close for the same species, or in this case, the petal length.

We'll use the `iris` dataset for this recipe:

```
>>> from sklearn import datasets
>>> iris = datasets.load_iris()
>>> iris.feature_names
['sepal length (cm)', 'sepal width (cm)', 'petal length (cm)',
 'petal width (cm)']
```

We'll try to predict the petal length based on the sepal length and width. We'll also fit a regular linear regression to see how well the k-NN regression does in comparison:

```
>>> from sklearn.linear_model import LinearRegression
>>> lr = LinearRegression()
>>> lr.fit(X, y)
>>> print "The MSE is: {:.2}".format(np.power(y - lr.predict(X),
            2).mean())
The MSE is: 0.15
```

Now, for the k-NN regression, use the following code:

```
>>> from sklearn.neighbors import KNeighborsRegressor
>>> knnr = KNeighborsRegressor(n_neighbors=10)
>>> knnr.fit(X, y)
>>> print "The MSE is: {:.2}".format(np.power(y - knnr.predict(X),
            2).mean())
The MSE is: 0.069
```

Let's look at what the k-NN regression does when we tell it to use the closest 10 points for regression:

```
>>> f, ax = plt.subplots(nrows=2, figsize=(7, 10))

>>> ax[0].set_title("Predictions")

>>> ax[0].scatter(X[:, 0], X[:, 1], s=lr.predict(X)*80, label='LR
    Predictions', color='c', edgecolors='black')
>>> ax[1].scatter(X[:, 0], X[:, 1], s=knnr.predict(X)*80, label='k-NN
    Predictions', color='m', edgecolors='black')

>>> ax[0].legend()
>>> ax[1].legend()
```

The following is the output:

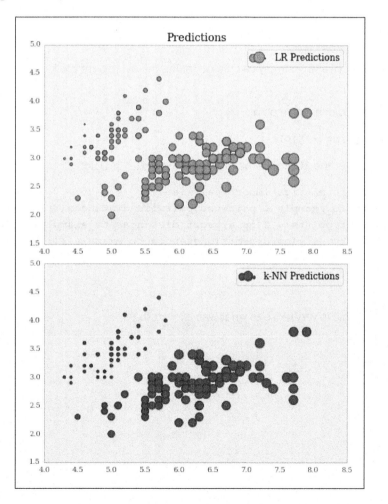

It might be completely clear that the predictions are close for the most part, but let's look at the predictions for the Setosa species as compared to the actuals:

```
>>> setosa_idx = np.where(iris.target_names=='setosa')
>>> setosa_mask = iris.target == setosa_idx[0]
>>> y[setosa_mask][:5]
array([ 0.2,  0.2,  0.2,  0.2,  0.2])
>>> knnr.predict(X)[setosa_mask][:5]
array([ 0.28,  0.17,  0.21,  0.2 ,  0.31])

>>> lr.predict(X)[setosa_mask][:5]
array([ 0.44636645, 0.53893889, 0.29846368, 0.27338255, 0.32612885])
```

Looking at the plots again, the Setosa species (upper-left cluster) is largely overestimated by linear regression, and k-NN is fairly close to the actual values.

## How it works...

The k-NN regression is very simply calculated taking the average of the k closest point to the point being tested.

Let's manually predict a single point:

```
>>> example_point = X[0]
```

Now, we need to get the 10 closest points to our example_point:

```
>>> from sklearn.metrics import pairwise
>>> distances_to_example = pairwise.pairwise_distances(X)[0]
>>> ten_closest_points = X[np.argsort(distances_to_example)][:10]
>>> ten_closest_y = y[np.argsort(distances_to_example)][:10]

>>> ten_closest_y.mean()
0.28000
```

We can see that this is very close to what was expected.

# 4
# Classifying Data with scikit-learn

This chapter will cover the following topics:

- ▶ Doing basic classifications with Decision Trees
- ▶ Tuning a Decision Tree model
- ▶ Using many Decisions Trees – random forests
- ▶ Tuning a random forest model
- ▶ Classifying data with support vector machines
- ▶ Generalizing with multiclass classification
- ▶ Using LDA for classification
- ▶ Working with QDA – a nonlinear LDA
- ▶ Using Stochastic Gradient Descent for classification
- ▶ Classifying documents with Naïve Bayes
- ▶ Label propagation with semi-supervised learning

## Introduction

Classification can be very important in a lot of contexts. For example, if we want to automate some decision-making process, we can utilize classification. In cases where we need to investigate a fraud, there are so many transactions that it is impractical for a person to check all of them. Therefore, we can automate such decisions with classification.

# Doing basic classifications with Decision Trees

In this recipe, we will perform basic classifications using Decision Trees. These are very nice models because they are easily understandable, and once trained in, scoring is very simple. Often, SQL statements can be used, which means that the outcome can be used by a lot of people.

## Getting ready

In this recipe, we'll look at Decision Trees. I like to think of Decision Trees as the base class from which a large number of other classification methods are derived. It's a pretty simple idea that works well in a bunch of situations.

First, let's get some classification data that we can practice on:

```
>>> from sklearn import datasets
>>> X, y = datasets.make_classification(n_samples=1000, n_features=3,
                                         n_redundant=0)
```

## How to do it...

Working with Decision Trees is easy. We first need to import the object, and then fit the model:

```
>>> from sklearn.tree import DecisionTreeClassifier
>>> dt = DecisionTreeClassifier()
>>> dt.fit(X, y)
DecisionTreeClassifier(compute_importances=None, criterion='gini',
                max_depth=None, max_features=None,
                max_leaf_nodes=None, min_density=None,
                min_samples_leaf=1, min_samples_split=2,
                random_state=None, splitter='best')

>>> preds = dt.predict(X)
>>> (y == preds).mean()
1.0
```

As you can see, we guessed it right. Clearly, this was just a dry run, now let's investigate some of our options.

First, if you look at the dt object, it has several keyword arguments that determine how the object will behave. How we choose the object is important, so we'll look at the object's effects in detail.

The first detail we'll look at is max_depth. This is an important parameter. It determines how many branches are allowed. This is important because a Decision Tree can have a hard time generalizing out-of-sampled data with some sort of regularization. Later, we'll see how we can use several shallow Decision Trees to make a better learner. Let's create a more complex dataset and see what happens when we allow different max_depth. We'll use this dataset for the rest of the recipe:

```
>>> n_features=200
>>> X, y = datasets.make_classification(750, n_features,
                                        n_informative=5)
>>> import numpy as np
>>> training = np.random.choice([True, False], p=[.75, .25],
                                size=len(y))

>>> accuracies = []

>>> for x in np.arange(1, n_features+1):
>>> dt = DecisionTreeClassifier(max_depth=x)

>>> dt.fit(X[training], y[training])

>>> preds = dt.predict(X[~training])

>>> accuracies.append((preds == y[~training]).mean())

>>> import matplotlib.pyplot as plt

>>> f, ax = plt.subplots(figsize=(7, 5))

>>> ax.plot(range(1, n_features+1), accuracies, color='k')

>>> ax.set_title("Decision Tree Accuracy")
>>> ax.set_ylabel("% Correct")
>>> ax.set_xlabel("Max Depth")
```

The following is the output:

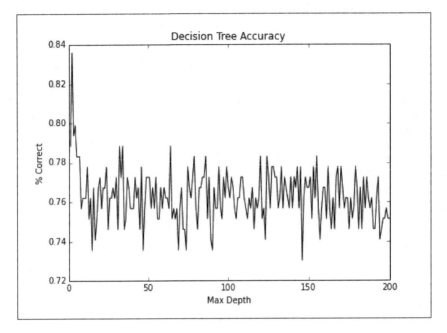

We can see that we actually get pretty accurate at a low max depth. Let's take a closer look at the accuracy at low levels, say the first 15:

```
>>> N = 15
>>> import matplotlib.pyplot as plt
>>> f, ax = plt.subplots(figsize=(7, 5))

>>> ax.plot(range(1, n_features+1)[:N], accuracies[:N], color='k')

>>> ax.set_title("Decision Tree Accuracy")
>>> ax.set_ylabel("% Correct")
>>> ax.set_xlabel("Max Depth")
```

The following is the output:

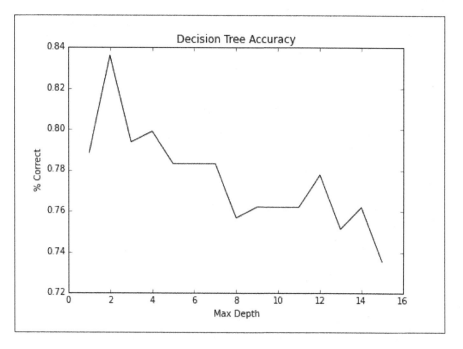

There's the spike we saw earlier; it's quite amazing to see the quick drop though. It's more likely that **Max Depth** of 1 through 3 is fairly equivalent. Decision Trees are quite good at separating rules, but they need to be reigned in.

We'll look at the `compute_importances` parameter here. It actually has a bit of a broader meaning for random forests, but we'll get acquainted with it. It's also worth noting that if you're using Version 0.16 or earlier, you will get this for free:

```
>>> dt_ci = DecisionTreeClassifier(compute_importances=True)
>>> dt.fit(X, y)

#plot the importances
>>> ne0 = dt.feature_importances_ != 0

>>> y_comp = dt.feature_importances_[ne0]
>>> x_comp = np.arange(len(dt.feature_importances_))[ne0]

>>> import matplotlib.pyplot as plt

>>> f, ax = plt.subplots(figsize=(7, 5))
>>> ax.bar(x_comp, y_comp)
```

The following is the output:

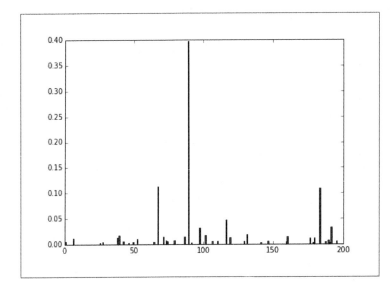

 Please note that you may get an error letting you know you'll no longer need to explicitly set compute importances.

As we can see, one of the features is by far the most important; several other features will follow up.

## How it works...

In the simplest sense, we construct Decision Trees all the time. When thinking through situations and assigning probabilities to outcomes, we construct Decision Trees. Our rules are much more complex and involve a lot of context, but with Decision Trees, all we care about is the difference between outcomes, given that some information is already known about a feature.

Now, let's discuss the differences between **entropy** and **Gini impurity**.

Entropy is more than just the entropy value at any given variable; it states what the change in entropy is if we know an element's value. This is called **Information Gain (IG)**; mathematically it looks like the following:

$$IG(\text{Data, Known Features}) = H(\text{Data}) - H(\text{Data}|\text{Known Features})$$

For **Gini impurity**, we care about how likely one of the data points will be mislabeled given the new information.

Both entropy and Gini impurity have pros and cons; this said, if you see major differences in the working of entropy and Gini impurity, it will probably be a good idea to re-examine your assumptions.

# Tuning a Decision Tree model

If we use just the basic implementation of a Decision Tree, it will probably not fit very well. Therefore, we need to tweak the parameters in order to get a good fit. This is very easy and won't require much effort.

## Getting ready

In this recipe, we will take an in-depth look at what it takes to tune a Decision Tree classifier. There are several options, and in the previous recipe, we only looked at one of these options.

We'll fit a basic model and actually look at what the Decision Tree looks like. Then, we'll re-examine after each decision and point out how various changes have influenced the structure.

If you want to follow along in this recipe, you'll need to install **pydot**.

## How to do it...

Decision Trees have a lot more "knobs" when compared to most other algorithms, because of which it's easier to see what happens when we turn the knobs:

```
>>> from sklearn import datasets
>>> X, y = datasets.make_classification(1000, 20, n_informative=3)

>>> from sklearn.tree import DecisionTreeClassifier
>>> dt = DecisionTreeClassifier()
>>> dt.fit(X, y)
```

Ok, so now that we have a basic classifier fit, we can view it quite simply:

```
>>> from StringIO import StringIO
>>> from sklearn import tree
>>> import pydot

>>> str_buffer = StringIO()
>>> tree.export_graphviz(dt, out_file=str_buffer)
>>> graph = pydot.graph_from_dot_data(str_buffer.getvalue())
>>> graph.write("myfile.jpg")
```

The graph is almost certainly illegible, but hopefully this illustrates the complex trees that can be generated as a result of using an unoptimized decision tree:

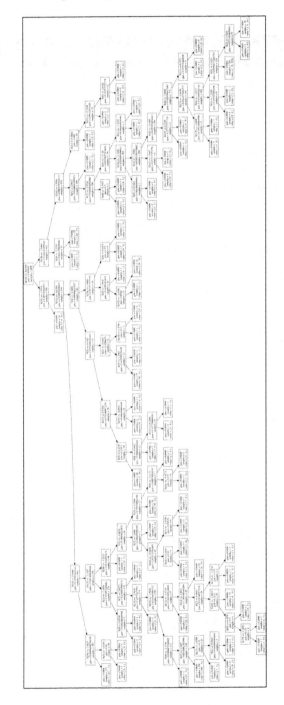

Wow! This is a very complex tree. It will most likely overfit the data. First, let's reduce the max depth value:

```
>>> dt = DecisionTreeClassifier(max_depth=5)
>>> dt.fit(X, y);
```

As an aside, if you're wondering why the semicolon, the `repr` by default, is seen, it is actually the model for a Decision Tree. For example, the `fit` function actually returns the Decision Tree object that allows chaining:

```
>>> dt = DecisionTreeClassifier(max_depth=5).fit(X, y)
```

Now, let's get back to the regularly scheduled program.

As we will plot this a few times, let's create a function:

```
>>> def plot_dt(model, filename):
        str_buffer = StringIO()
>>> tree.export_graphviz(model, out_file=str_buffer)

>>> graph = pydot.graph_from_dot_data(str_buffer.getvalue())
>>> graph.write_jpg(filename)

>>> plot_dt(dt, "myfile.png")
```

The following is the graph that will be generated:

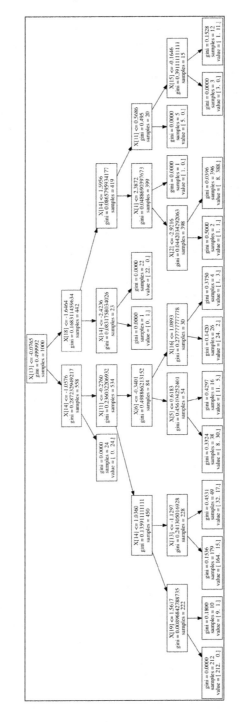

This is a much simpler tree. Let's look at what happens when we use entropy as the splitting criteria:

```
>>> dt = DecisionTreeClassifier(criterion='entropy',
                                max_depth=5).fit(X, y)
>>> plot(dt, "entropy.png")
```

The following is the graph that can be generated:

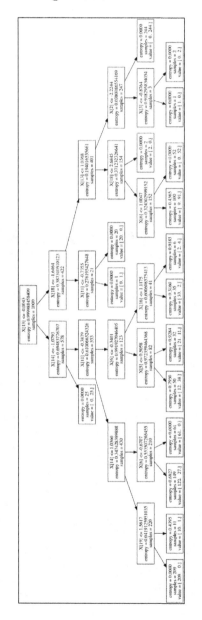

It's good to see that the first two splits are the same features, and the first few after this are interspersed with similar amounts. This is a good sanity check.

Also, note how entropy for the first split is 0.999, but for the first split when using the Gini impurity is 0.5. This has to do with how different the two measures of the split of a Decision Tree are. See the following *How it works...* section for more information. However, if we want to create a Decision Tree with entropy, we must use the following command:

```
>>> dt = DecisionTreeClassifier(min_samples_leaf=10,
                                criterion='entropy',
                                max_depth=5).fit(X, y)
```

## How it works...

Decision Trees, in general, suffer from overfitting. Quite often, left to it's own devices, a Decision Tree model will overfit, and therefore, we need to think about how best to avoid overfitting; this is done to avoid complexity. A simple model will more often work better in practice than not.

We're about to see this very idea in practice. random forests will build on this idea of simple models.

# Using many Decision Trees – random forests

In this recipe, we'll use random forests for classification tasks. random forests are used because they're very robust to overfitting and perform well in a variety of situations.

## Getting ready

We'll explore this more in the *How it works...* section of this recipe, but random forests work by constructing a lot of very shallow trees, and then taking a vote of the class that each tree "voted" for. This idea is very powerful in machine learning. If we recognize that a simple trained classifier might only be 60 percent accurate, we can train lots of classifiers that are generally right and can then use the learners together.

## How to do it...

The mechanics of training a random forest classifier is very easy with scikit-learn. In this section, we'll do the following:

1. Create a sample dataset to practice with.
2. Train a basic random forest object.
3. Take a look at some of the attributes of a trained object.

In the next recipe, we'll look at how to tune the random forest classifier. Let's start by importing datasets:

```
>>> from sklearn import datasets
```

Then, create the dataset with 1,000 samples:

```
>>> X, y = datasets.make_classification(1000)
```

Now that we have the data, we can create a classifier object and train it:

```
>>> from sklearn.ensemble import RandomForestClassifier

>>> rf = RandomForestClassifier()

>>> rf.fit(X, y)
```

The first thing we want to do is see how well we fit the training data. We can use the `predict` method for these projections:

```
>>> print "Accuracy:\t", (y == rf.predict(X)).mean()
Accuracy:    0.993

>>> print "Total Correct:\t", (y == rf.predict(X)).sum()
Total Correct:    993
```

Now, let's look at some attributes and methods.

First, we'll look at some of the useful attributes; in this case, since we used defaults, they'll be the object defaults:

- ▶ `rf.criterion`: This is the criterion for how the splits are determined. The default is `gini`.
- ▶ `rf.bootstrap`: A Boolean that indicates whether we used bootstrap samples when training random forest.
- ▶ `rf.n_jobs`: The number of jobs to train and predict. If you want to use all the processors, set this to `-1`. Keep in mind that if your dataset isn't very big, it often leads to more overhead in using multiple jobs due to the data having to be serialized and moved in between processes.
- ▶ `rf.max_features`: This denotes the number of features to consider when making the best split. This will come in handy during the tuning process.
- ▶ `rf.compute_importances`: This helps us decide whether to compute the importance of the features. See the *There's more...* section of this recipe for information on how to use this.
- ▶ `rf.max_depth`: This denotes how deep each tree can go.

There are more attributes to note; check out the official documentation for more details.

The `predict` method isn't the only useful one. We can also get the probabilities of each class from individual samples. This can be a useful feature to understand the uncertainty in each prediction. For instance, we can predict the probabilities of each sample for the various classes:

```
>>> probs = rf.predict_proba(X)

>>> import pandas as pd

>>> probs_df = pd.DataFrame(probs, columns=['0', '1'])
>>> probs_df['was_correct'] = rf.predict(X) == y

>>> import matplotlib.pyplot as plt

>>> f, ax = plt.subplots(figsize=(7, 5))

>>> probs_df.groupby('0').was_correct.mean().plot(kind='bar', ax=ax)
>>> ax.set_title("Accuracy at 0 class probability")
>>> ax.set_ylabel("% Correct")
>>> ax.set_xlabel("% trees for 0")
```

The following is the output:

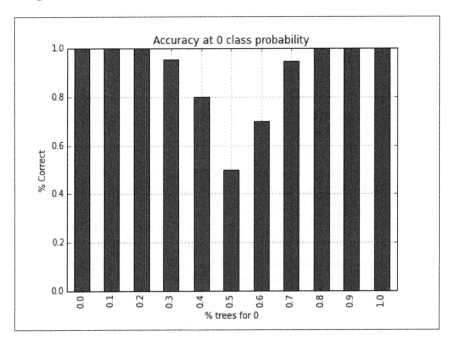

## How it works...

Random forest works by using a predetermined number of weak Decision Trees and by training each one of these trees on a subset of data. This is critical in avoiding overfitting. This is also the reason for the `bootstrap` parameter. We have each tree trained with the following:

- The class with the most votes
- The output, if we use regression trees

There are, of course, performance considerations, which we'll cover in the next recipe, but for the purposes of understanding how random forests work, we train a bunch of average trees and get a fairly good classifier as a result.

## There's more...

Feature importance is a good by-product of random forests. This often helps to answer the question: *If we have 10 features, which features are most important in determining the true class of the data point?* The real-world applications are hopefully easy to see. For example, if a transaction is fraudulent, we probably want to know if there are certain signals that can be used to figure out a transaction's class more quickly.

If we want to calculate the feature importance, we need to state it when we create the object. If you use scikit-learn 0.15, you might get a warning that it is not required; in Version 0.16, the warning will be removed:

```
>>> rf = RandomForestClassifier(compute_importances=True)
>>> rf.fit(X, y)
>>> f, ax = plt.subplots(figsize=(7, 5))
>>> ax.bar(range(len(rf.feature_importances_)),
           rf.feature_importances_)
>>> ax.set_title("Feature Importances")
```

The following is the output:

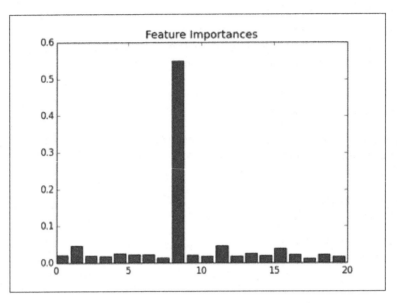

As we can see, certain features are much more important than others when determining if the outcome was of class 0 or class 1.

# Tuning a random forest model

In the previous recipe, we reviewed how to use the random forest classifier. In this recipe, we'll walk through how to tune its performance by tuning its parameters.

## Getting ready

In order to tune a random forest model, we'll need to first create a dataset that's a little more difficult to predict. Then, we'll alter the parameters and do some preprocessing to fit the dataset better.

So, let's create the dataset first:

```
>>> from sklearn import datasets
>>> X, y = datasets.make_classification(n_samples=10000,
                          n_features=20,
                          n_informative=15,
                          flip_y=.5, weights=[.2, .8])
```

## How to do it...

In this recipe, we will do the following:

1. Create a training and test set. We won't just sail through this recipe like we did in the previous recipe. It's an empty deed to tune a model without comparing it to a training set.

2. Fit a baseline random forest to evaluate how well we do with a naive algorithm.

3. Alter some parameters in a systematic way, and then observe what happens to the fit.

Ok, start an interpreter and import NumPy:

```
>>> import numpy as np
>>> training = np.random.choice([True, False], p=[.8, .2],
                                size=y.shape)

>>> from sklearn.ensemble import RandomForestClassifier

>>> rf = RandomForestClassifier()
>>> rf.fit(X[training], y[training])

>>> preds = rf.predict(X[~training])

>>> print "Accuracy:\t", (preds == y[~training]).mean()
Accuracy:  0.652239557121
```

I'm going to cheat a little bit and introduce one of the model evaluation metrics we will talk about later in the book. Accuracy is a good first metric, but using a confusion matrix will help us understand what's going on.

Let's iterate through the recommended choices for `max_features` and see what it does to the fit. We'll also iterate through a couple of **floats**, which are the fraction of the features that will be used. Use the following commands to do so:

```
>>> from sklearn.metrics import confusion_matrix

>>> max_feature_params = ['auto', 'sqrt', 'log2', .01, .5, .99]

>>> confusion_matrixes = {}

>>> for max_feature in max_feature_params:
        rf = RandomForestClassifier(max_features=max_feature)
```

```
        rf.fit(X[training], y[training])

>>> confusion_matrixes[max_feature] = confusion_matrix(y[~training])

>>> rf.predict(X[~training])).ravel()
```

Since I used the `ravel` method, our 2D confusion matrices are now 1D.

Now, import pandas and look at the confusion matrix we just created:

```
>>> import pandas as pd

>>> confusion_df = pd.DataFrame(confusion_matrixes)

>>> import itertools
>>> from matplotlib import pyplot as plt
>>> f, ax = plt.subplots(figsize=(7, 5))

>>> confusion_df.plot(kind='bar', ax=ax)

>>> ax.legend(loc='best')

>>> ax.set_title("Guessed vs Correct (i, j) where i is the guess and j is
                  the actual.")

>>> ax.grid()

>>> ax.set_xticklabels([str((i, j)) for i, j in
                        list(itertools.product(range(2), range(2)))]);
>>> ax.set_xlabel("Guessed vs Correct")
>>> ax.set_ylabel("Correct")
```

The following is the output:

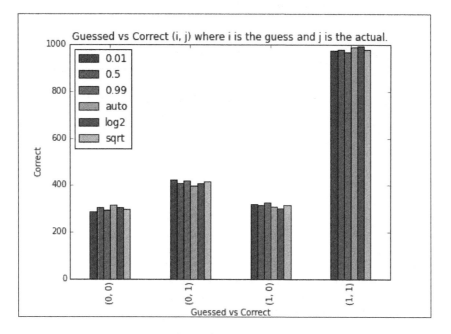

While we didn't see any real difference in performance, this is a fairly simple process to go through for your own projects. Let's try it on the choice of n_estimator instances, but use raw accuracy. With more than a few options, our graph is going to become very cloudy and difficult to use.

Since we're using the confusion matrix, we can get the accuracy from the trace of the confusion matrix divided by the overall sum:

```
>>> n_estimator_params = range(1, 20)

>>> confusion_matrixes = {}

>>> for n_estimator in n_estimator_params:
        rf = RandomForestClassifier(n_estimators=n_estimator)

        rf.fit(X[training], y[training])

        confusion_matrixes[n_estimator] = confusion_matrix(y[~training],
                                    rf.predict(X[~training]))
```

```
    # here's where we'll update the confusion matrix with the
      operation we talked about

>>> accuracy = lambda x: np.trace(x) / np.sum(x, dtype=float)
>>> confusion_matrixes[n_estimator] =
                        accuracy(confusion_matrixes[n_estimator])

>>> accuracy_series = pd.Series(confusion_matrixes)

>>> import itertools
>>> from matplotlib import pyplot as plt

>>> f, ax = plt.subplots(figsize=(7, 5))

>>> accuracy_series.plot(kind='bar', ax=ax, color='k', alpha=.75)
>>> ax.grid()

>>> ax.set_title("Accuracy by Number of Estimators")
>>> ax.set_ylim(0, 1) # we want the full scope
>>> ax.set_ylabel("Accuracy")
>>> ax.set_xlabel("Number of Estimators")
```

The following is the output:

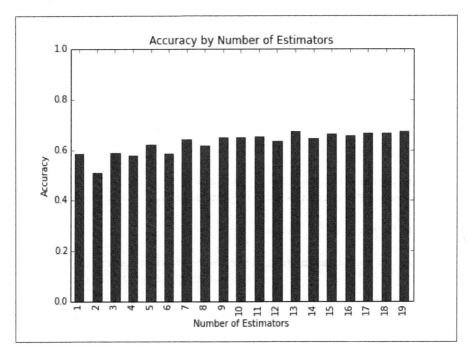

Notice how accuracy is going up for the most part. There certainly is some randomness associated with the accuracy, but the graph is up and to the right. In the following *How it works...* section, we'll talk about the association between random forest and bootstrap, and what is generally better.

## How it works...

Bootstrapping is a nice technique to augment the other parts of modeling. The case often used to introduce bootstrapping is adding standard errors to a median. Here, we just estimate the outcome over and over and aggregate the estimates up to probabilities.

So, by simply increasing the number estimators, we increase the subsamples that lead to an overall faster convergence.

## There's more...

We might want to speed up the training process. I alluded to this process earlier, but we can set n_jobs to the number of trees we want to train at the same time. This should roughly be the number of cores on the machine:

```
>>> rf = RandomForestClassifier(n_jobs=4, verbose=True)
>>> rf.fit(X, y)
[Parallel(n_jobs=4)]: Done   1 out of   4 | elapsed:   0.3s remaining: 0.9s
[Parallel(n_jobs=4)]: Done   4 out of   4 | elapsed:   0.3s finished
```

This will also predict in parallel (verbosely):

```
>>> rf.predict(X)
[Parallel(n_jobs=4)]: Done   1 out of   4 | elapsed:   0.0s remaining:
0.0s
[Parallel(n_jobs=4)]: Done   4 out of   4 | elapsed:   0.0s finished

array([1, 1, 0, ..., 1, 1, 1])
```

# Classifying data with support vector machines

**Support vector machines** (**SVM**) is one of the techniques we will use that doesn't have an easy probabilistic interpretation. The idea behind SVMs is that we find the plane that separates the group of the dataset the "best". Here, separation means that the choice of the plane maximizes the margin between the closest points on the plane. These points are called **support vectors**.

## Getting ready

SVM is one of my favorite machine learning algorithms. It was one of the first machine learning algorithms I learned in school. So, let's get some data and get started:

```
>>> from sklearn import datasets
>>> X, y = datasets.make_classification()
```

## How to do it...

The mechanics of creating a support vector classifier is very simple; there are a few options available. Therefore, we'll do the following:

1.  Create an SVC object and fit it to some fake data.
2.  Fit the SVC object to some example data.
3.  Talk a little about the SVC options.

Import **support vector classifier** (**SVC**) from the support vector machine module:

```
>>> from sklearn.svm import SVC

>>> base_svm = SVC()

>>> base_svm.fit(X, y)
```

Let's look at some of the attributes:

- ▸  C: In cases where we don't have a well-separated set, C will scale the error on the margin. As C gets higher, the penalization for the error becomes larger and the SVM will try to find a narrow margin even if it misclassifies more points.

- ▸  class_weight: This denotes how much weight to give to each class in the problem. This is given as a dictionary where classes are the keys and values are the weights associated with these classes.

- ▸ gamma: This is the gamma parameter for kernels and is supported by rgb, sigmoid, and ploy.

- ▸ kernel: This is the kernel to use; we'll use linear in the following *How it works...* section, but rgb is the popular and default choice.

## How it works...

Like we talked about in the *Getting ready* section, SVM will try to find the plane that best bifurcates the two classes. Let's look at a simple example with two features and a well-separated outcome.

First, let's fit the dataset, and then we'll plot what's going on:

```
>>> X, y = datasets.make_blobs(n_features=2, centers=2)
>>> from sklearn.svm import LinearSVC
>>> svm = LinearSVC()
>>> svm.fit(X, y)
```

Now that we've fit the support vector machine, we'll plot its outcome at each point in the graph. This will show us the approximate decision boundary:

```
>>> from itertools import product
>>> from collections import namedtuple

>>> Point = namedtuple('Point', ['x', 'y', 'outcome'])
>>> decision_boundary = []
>>> xmin, xmax = np.percentile(X[:, 0], [0, 100])
>>> ymin, ymax = np.percentile(X[:, 1], [0, 100])


>>> for xpt, ypt in product(np.linspace(xmin-2.5, xmax+2.5, 20),
        np.linspace(ymin-2.5, ymax+2.5, 20)):
            p = Point(xpt, ypt, svm.predict([xpt, ypt]))
            decision_boundary.append(p)

>>> import matplotlib.pyplot as plt
>>> f, ax = plt.subplots(figsize=(7, 5))
>>> import numpy as np
>>> colors = np.array(['r', 'b'])
>>> for xpt, ypt, pt in decision_boundary:
        ax.scatter(xpt, ypt, color=colors[pt[0]], alpha=.15)
        ax.scatter(X[:, 0], X[:, 1], color=colors[y], s=30)
        ax.set_ylim(ymin, ymax)
        ax.set_xlim(xmin, xmax)
        ax.set_title("A well separated dataset")
```

The following is the output:

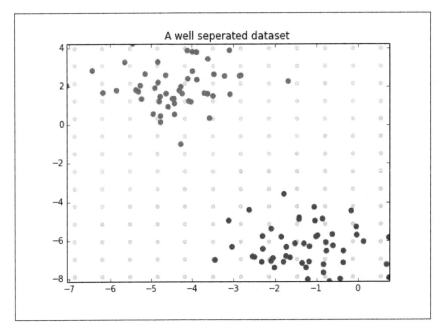

Let's look at another example, but this time the **decision boundary** will not be so clear:

```
>>> X, y = datasets.make_classification(n_features=2,
                                         n_classes=2,
                                         n_informative=2,
                                         n_redundant=0)
```

As we can see, this is not a problem that will easily be solved by a linear classification rule.

While we will not use this in practice, let's have a look at the decision boundary. First, let's retrain the classifier with the new datapoints:

```
>>> svm.fit(X, y)
>>> xmin, xmax = np.percentile(X[:, 0], [0, 100])
>>> ymin, ymax = np.percentile(X[:, 1], [0, 100])
>>> test_points = np.array([[xx, yy] for xx, yy in
                           product(np.linspace(xmin, xmax),
                           np.linspace(ymin, ymax))])
>>> test_preds = svm.predict(test_points)
```

```
>>> import matplotlib.pyplot as plt
>>> f, ax = plt.subplots(figsize=(7, 5))
>>> import numpy as np
>>> colors = np.array(['r', 'b'])
>>> ax.scatter(test_points[:, 0], test_points[:, 1],
               color=colors[test_preds], alpha=.25)
>>> ax.scatter(X[:, 0], X[:, 1], color=colors[y])
>>> ax.set_title("A well separated dataset")
```

The following is the output:

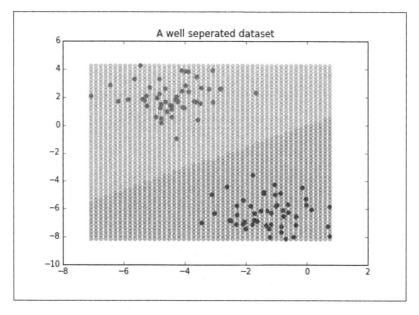

As we saw, the decision line isn't perfect, but at the end of the day, this is the best Linear SVM we will get.

## There's more...

While we might not be able to get a better Linear SVM by default, the SVC classifier in scikit-learn will use the radial basis function. We've seen this function before, but let's take a look and see what it does to the decision boundaries of the dataset we just fit:

```
>>> radial_svm = SVC(kernel='rbf')
>>> radial_svm.fit(X, y)
>>> xmin, xmax = np.percentile(X[:, 0], [0, 100])
>>> ymin, ymax = np.percentile(X[:, 1], [0, 100])
```

```
>>> test_points = np.array([[xx, yy] for xx, yy in
                            product(np.linspace(xmin, xmax),
                            np.linspace(ymin, ymax))])
>>> test_preds = radial_svm.predict(test_points)

>>> import matplotlib.pyplot as plt
>>> f, ax = plt.subplots(figsize=(7, 5))
>>> import numpy as np
>>> colors = np.array(['r', 'b'])
>>> ax.scatter(test_points[:, 0], test_points[:, 1],
            color=colors[test_preds], alpha=.25)
>>> ax.scatter(X[:, 0], X[:, 1], color=colors[y])
>>> ax.set_title("SVM with a radial basis function")
```

The following is the output:

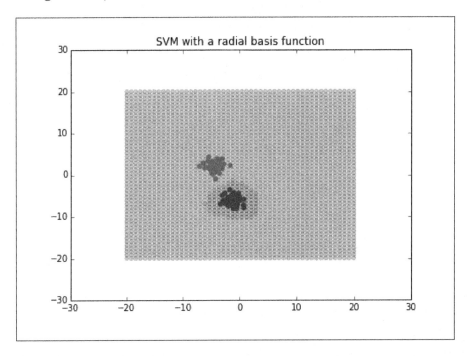

As we can see, the decision boundary has been altered. We can even pass in our own radial basis function, if needed:

```
>>> def test_kernel(X, y):
        """ Test kernel that returns the exponentiation of the dot of the
        X and y matrices.
```

This looks an awful lot like the log hazards if you're familiar with survival analysis.
```
    """
    return np.exp(np.dot(X, y.T))
>>> test_svc = SVC(kernel=test_kernel)
>>> test_svc.fit(X, y)
SVC(C=1.0, cache_size=200, class_weight=None, coef0=0.0, degree=3,
    gamma=0.0,   kernel=<function test_kernel at 0x121fdfb90>,
    max_iter=-1,   probability=False, random_state=None,
    shrinking=True, tol=0.001,   verbose=False)
```

# Generalizing with multiclass classification

In this recipe, we'll look at multiclass classification. Depending on your choice of algorithm, you either get multiclass classification for free, or you have to define a scheme for comparison.

## Getting ready

When working with linear models such as logistic regression, we need to use `OneVsRestClassifier`. This scheme will create a classifier for each class.

## How to do it...

First, we'll walk through a cursory example of a Decision Tree fitting a multiclass dataset. Like we discussed earlier, we get multiclass for free with some classifiers, so we'll just fit the example to prove that it works, and move on.

Second, we'll actually incorporate `OneVsRestClassifier` into our model:

```
>>> from sklearn import datasets
>>> X, y = datasets.make_classification(n_samples=10000, n_classes=3,
                                     n_informative=3)

>>> from sklearn.tree import DecisionTreeClassifier
>>> dt = DecisionTreeClassifier()
>>> dt.fit(X, y)
>>> dt.predict(X)
array([1, 1, 0, .., 2, 1, 1])
```

As you can see, we were able to fit a classifier with minimum effort.

Now, let's move on to the case of the multiclass classifier. This will require us to import `OneVsRestClassifier`. We'll also import `LogisticRegression` while we're at it:

```
>>> from sklearn.multiclass import OneVsRestClassifier
>>> from sklearn.linear_model import LogisticRegression
```

Now, we'll override the `LogisticRegression` classifier. Also, notice that we can parallelize this. If we think about how `OneVsRestClassifier` works, it's just training separate models and then comparing them. So, we can train the data separately at the same time:

```
>>> mlr = OneVsRestClassifier(LogisticRegression(), n_jobs=2)
>>> mlr.fit(X, y)
>>> mlr.predict(X)
array([1, 1, 0, ..., 2, 1, 1])
```

## How it works...

If we want to quickly create our own `OneVsRestClassifier`, how might we do it?

First, we need to construct a way to iterate through the classes and train a classifier for each classifier. Then, we need to predict each class first:

```
>>> import numpy as np
>>> def train_one_vs_rest(y, class_label):
        y_train = (y == class_label).astype(int)
        return y_train

>>> classifiers = []
>>> for class_i in sorted(np.unique(y)):
        l = LogisticRegression()
        y_train = train_one_vs_rest(y, class_i)
        l.fit(X, y_train)
        classifiers.append(l)
```

Ok, so now that we have a one versus rest scheme set up, all we need to do is evaluate the data point's likelihood for each classifier. We will then assign the classifier to the data point with the largest likelihood.

For example, let's predict X[0]:

```
for classifier in classifiers
>>>    print classifier.predict_proba(X[0])

[[ 0.90443776  0.09556224]]
[[ 0.03701073  0.96298927]]
[[ 0.98492829  0.01507171]]
```

As you can see, the second classifier (the one in index 1) has the highest likelihood of being "positive", therefore we'll assign 1 to this point.

# Using LDA for classification

**Linear Discriminant Analysis** (**LDA**) attempts to fit a linear combination of features to predict the outcome variable. LDA is often used as a preprocessing step. We'll walk through both methods in this recipe.

## Getting ready

In this recipe, we will do the following:

1. Grab stock data from Yahoo.

2. Rearrange it in a shape we're comfortable with.

3. Create an LDA object to fit and predict the class labels.

4. Give an example of how to use LDA for dimensionality reduction.

## How to do it...

In this example, we will perform an analysis similar to **Altman's Z-score**. In this paper, Altman looked at a company's likelihood of defaulting within two years based on several financial metrics. The following is taken from the Wiki page of Altman's Z-score:

$T_1$ = *Working Capital / Total Assets. Measures liquid assets in relation to the size of the company.*

$T_2$ = *Retained Earnings / Total Assets. Measures profitability that reflects the company's age and earning power.*

$T_3$ = *Earnings Before Interest and Taxes / Total Assets. Measures operating efficiency apart from tax and leveraging factors. It recognizes operating earnings as being important to long-term viability.*

$T_4$ = *Market Value of Equity / Book Value of Total Liabilities. Adds market dimension that can show up security price fluctuation as a possible red flag.*

$T_5$ = *Sales/ Total Assets. Standard measure for total asset turnover (varies greatly from industry to industry).*

From Wikipedia:

[1]: Altman, Edward I. (September 1968). ""Financial Ratios, Discriminant Analysis and the Prediction of Corporate Bankruptcy"". Journal of Finance: 189–209.

In this analysis, we'll look at some financial data from Yahoo via pandas. We'll try to predict if a stock will be higher in exactly 6 months from today, based on the current attribute of the stock. It's obviously nowhere near as refined as Altman's Z-score. Let's use a basket of auto stocks:

```
>>> tickers = ["F", "TM", "GM", "TSLA"]
>>> from pandas.io import data as external_data
>>> stock_panel = external_data.DataReader(tickers, "yahoo")
```

This data structure is `panel` from pandas. It's similar to an OLAP cube or a 3D `DataFrame`. Let's take a look at the data to get some familiarity with closes since that's what we care about while comparing:

```
>>> stock_df = stock_panel.Close.dropna()
>>> stock_df.plot(figsize=(7, 5))
```

The following is the output:

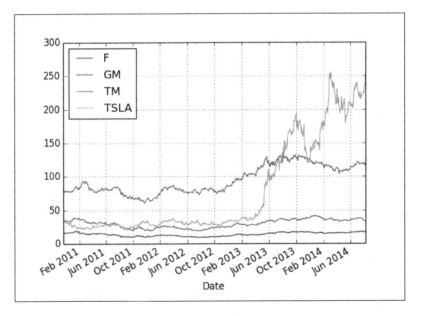

Ok, so now we need to compare each stock price with its price in 6 months. If it's higher, we'll code it with 1, and if not, we'll code that with 0.

To do this, we'll just shift the dataframe back 180 days and compare:

```
#this dataframe indicates if the stock was higher in 180 days
>>> classes = (stock_df.shift(-180) > stock_df).astype(int)
```

The next thing we need to do is flatten out the dataset:

```
>>> X = stock_panel.to_frame()
>>> classes = classes.unstack()
>>> classes = classes.swaplevel(0, 1).sort_index()
>>> classes = classes.to_frame()
>>> classes.index.names = ['Date', 'minor']
>>> data = X.join(classes).dropna()
>>> data.rename(columns={0: 'is_higher'}, inplace=True)
>>> data.head()
```

The following is the output:

| Date | minor | Open | High | Low | Close | Volume | Adj Close | is_higher |
|---|---|---|---|---|---|---|---|---|
| 2010-11-18 | F | 16.77 | 16.87 | 16.05 | 16.12 | 256937900 | 15.07 | 0 |
| | GM | 35.00 | 35.99 | 33.89 | 34.19 | 457044300 | 33.61 | 0 |
| | TM | 77.36 | 77.51 | 76.83 | 77.29 | 989100 | 77.29 | 0 |
| | TSLA | 30.67 | 30.74 | 28.92 | 29.89 | 956100 | 29.89 | 0 |
| 2010-11-19 | F | 16.02 | 16.38 | 15.83 | 16.28 | 130323600 | 15.22 | 0 |

Ok, so now we need to create matrices to SciPy. To do this, we'll use the `patsy` library. This is a great library that can be used to create a design matrix in a fashion similar to R:

```
>>> import patsy
>>> X = patsy.dmatrix("Open + High + Low + Close + Volume +
                      is_higher - 1", data.reset_index(),
                      return_type='dataframe')
>>> X.head()
```

The following is the output:

|   | Open | High | Low | Close | Volume | is_higher |
|---|------|------|------|-------|--------|-----------|
| 0 | 16.77 | 16.87 | 16.05 | 16.12 | 256937900 | 0 |
| 1 | 35.00 | 35.99 | 33.89 | 34.19 | 457044300 | 0 |
| 2 | 77.36 | 77.51 | 76.83 | 77.29 | 989100 | 0 |
| 3 | 30.67 | 30.74 | 28.92 | 29.89 | 956100 | 0 |
| 4 | 16.02 | 16.38 | 15.83 | 16.28 | 130323600 | 0 |

`patsy` is a very strong package, for example, suppose we want to apply some of the preprocessing from *Chapter 1, Premodel Workflow*. In `patsy`, it's possible, like in R, to modify the formula in a way that corresponds to modifications in the design matrix. It won't be done here, but if we want to scale the value to mean 0 and standard deviation 1, the function will be `"scale(open) + scale(high)"`.

Awesome! So, now that we have our dataset, let's fit the LDA object:

```
>>> import pandas as pd
>>> from sklearn.lda import LDA
>>> lda = LDA()
>>> lda.fit(X.ix[:, :-1], X.ix[:, -1]);
```

We can see that it's not too bad when predicting against the dataset. Certainly, we will want to improve this with other parameters and test the model:

```
>>> from sklearn.metrics import classification_report
>>> print classification_report(X.ix[:, -1].values,
                        lda.predict(X.ix[:, :-1]))
              precision    recall    f1-score    support
0.0                0.63      0.59        0.61       1895
1.0                0.60      0.64        0.62       1833
avg / total        0.61      0.61        0.61       3728
```

These metrics describe how the model fits the data in various ways.

The `precision` and `recall` parameters are fairly similar. In some ways, as shown in the following list, they can be thought of as conditional proportions:

- For `precision`, given the model predicts a positive value, what proportion of this is correct?

- For `recall`, given the state of one class is true, what proportion did we "select"? I say, select because recall is a common metric in search problems. For example, there can be a set of underlying web pages that, in fact, relate to a search term—the proportion that is returned.

The `f1-score` parameter attempts to summarize the relationship between `recall` and `precision`.

## How it works...

LDA is actually fairly similar to clustering that we did previously. We fit a basic model from the data. Then, once we have the model, we try to predict and compare the likelihoods of the data given in each class. We choose the option that's more likely.

LDA is actually a simplification of QDA, which we'll talk about in the next chapter. Here, we assume that the covariance of each class is the same, but in QDA, the assumption is relaxed. Think about the connections between KNN and GMM and the relationship there and here.

# Working with QDA – a nonlinear LDA

QDA is the generalization of a common technique such as quadratic regression. It is simply a generalization of the model to allow for more complex models to fit, though, like all things, when allowing complexity to creep in, we make our life more difficult.

## Getting ready

We will expand on the last recipe and look at **Quadratic Discernment Analysis (QDA)** via the QDA object.

We said we made an assumption about the covariance of the model. Here, we will relax the assumption.

## How to do it...

QDA is aptly a member of the `qda` module. Use the following commands to use QDA:

```
>>> from sklearn.qda import QDA
>>> qda = QDA()

>>> qda.fit(X.ix[:, :-1], X.ix[:, -1])
>>> predictions = qda.predict(X.ix[:, :-1])
>>> predictions.sum()
2812.0

>>> from sklearn.metrics import classification_report
>>> print classification_report(X.ix[:, -1].values, predictions)
```

| | precision | recall | f1-score | support |
|---|---|---|---|---|
| 0.0 | 0.75 | 0.36 | 0.49 | 1895 |
| 1.0 | 0.57 | 0.88 | 0.69 | 1833 |
| avg / total | 0.66 | 0.62 | 0.59 | 3728 |

As you can see, it's about equal on the whole. If we look back at the LDA recipe, we can see large changes as opposed to the QDA object for class 0 and minor differences for class 1.

## How it works...

Like we talked about in the last recipe, we essentially compare likelihoods here. So, how do we compare likelihoods? Let's just use the price at hand to attempt to classify is_higher.

We'll assume that the closing price is log-normally distributed. In order to compute the likelihood for each class, we need to create the subsets of closes as well as a training and test set for each class. As a sneak peak to the next chapter, we'll use the built-in cross validation methods:

```
>>> from sklearn import cross_validation as cv

>>> import scipy.stats as sp

>>> for test, train in cv.ShuffleSplit(len(X.Close), n_iter=1):
        train_set = X.iloc[train]
        train_close = train_set.Close

        train_0 = train_close[~train_set.is_higher.astype(bool)]
        train_1 = train_close[train_set.is_higher.astype(bool)]

        test_set = X.iloc[test]
        test_close = test_set.Close.values

        ll_0 = sp.norm.pdf(test_close, train_0.mean())
        ll_1 = sp.norm.pdf(test_close, train_1.mean())
```

Now that we have likelihoods for both classes, we can compare and assign classes:

```
>>> (ll_0 > ll_1).mean()
0.15588673621460505
```

# Using Stochastic Gradient Descent for classification

As was discussed in *Chapter 2, Working with Linear Models*, Stochastic Gradient Descent is a fundamental technique to fit a model for regression. There are natural connections between the two techniques, as the name so obviously implies.

## Getting ready

In regression, we minimized a cost function that penalized for bad choices on a continuous scale, but for classification, we'll minimize a cost function that penalizes for two (or more) cases.

## How to do it...

First, let's create some very basic data:

```
>>> from sklearn import datasets
>>> X, y = datasets.make_classification()
```

Next, we'll create a SGDClassifier instance:

```
>>> from sklearn import linear_model
>>> sgd_clf = linear_model.SGDClassifier()
```

As usual, we'll fit the model:

```
>>> sgd_clf.fit(X, y)
SGDClassifier(alpha=0.0001, class_weight=None, epsilon=0.1, eta0=0.0,
              fit_intercept=True, l1_ratio=0.15,
              learning_rate='optimal', loss='hinge', n_iter=5,
              n_jobs=1, penalty='l2', power_t=0.5, random_state=None,
              shuffle=False, verbose=0, warm_start=False)
```

We can set the class_weight parameter to account for the varying amounts of unbalance in a dataset.

The Hinge loss function is defined as follows:

$$\max(0, 1 - ty)$$

Here, t is the true classification denoted as +1 for one case and -1 for the other. The vector of coefficients is denoted by y as fit from the model, and x is the value of interest. There is also an intercept for good measure. To put it another way:

$$t \in -1, 1$$

$$y = \beta x + b$$

# Classifying documents with Naïve Bayes

Naïve Bayes is a really interesting model. It's somewhat similar to k-NN in the sense that it makes some assumptions that might oversimplify reality, but still perform well in many cases.

## Getting ready

In this recipe, we'll use Naïve Bayes to do document classification with sklearn. An example I have personal experience of is using the words that make up an account descriptor in accounting, such as Accounts Payable, and determining if it belongs to Income Statement, Cash Flow Statement, or Balance Sheet.

The basic idea is to use the word frequency from a labeled test corpus to learn the classifications of the documents. Then, we can turn this on a training set and attempt to predict the label.

We'll use the `newgroups` dataset within sklearn to play with the Naïve Bayes model. It's a nontrivial amount of data, so we'll fetch it instead of loading it. We'll also limit the categories to `rec.autos` and `rec.motorcycles`:

```
>>> from sklearn.datasets import fetch_20newsgroups

>>> categories = ["rec.autos", "rec.motorcycles"]
>>> newgroups = fetch_20newsgroups(categories=categories)


#take a look
>>> print "\n".join(newgroups.data[:1])
From: gregl@zimmer.CSUFresno.EDU (Greg Lewis)
Subject: Re: WARNING.....(please read)...
Keywords: BRICK, TRUCK, DANGER
Nntp-Posting-Host: zimmer.csufresno.edu
Organization: CSU Fresno
Lines: 33
```

[...]

```
>>> newgroups.target_names[newgroups.target[:1]]
'rec.autos'
```

Now that we have `newgroups`, we'll need to represent each document as a bag of words. This representation is what gives Naïve Bayes its name. The model is "naive" because documents are classified without regard for any intradocument word covariance. This might be considered a flaw, but Naïve Bayes has been shown to work reasonably well.

We need to preprocess the data into a bag-of-words matrix. This is a sparse matrix that has entries when the word is present in the document. This matrix can become quite large, as illustrated:

```
>>> from sklearn.feature_extraction.text import CountVectorizer
```

```
>>> count_vec = CountVectorizer()
>>> bow = count_vec.fit_transform(newgroups.data)
```

This matrix is a sparse matrix, which is the length of the number of documents by each word. The document and word value of the matrix are the frequency of the particular term:

```
>>> bow
<1192x19177 sparse matrix of type '<type 'numpy.int64'>'
    with 164296 stored elements in Compressed Sparse Row format>
```

We'll actually need the matrix as a dense array for the Naïve Bayes object. So, let's convert it back:

```
>>> bow = np.array(bow.todense())
```

Clearly, most of the entries are 0, but we might want to reconstruct the document counts as a sanity check:

```
>>> words = np.array(count_vec.get_feature_names())
>>> words[bow[0] > 0][:5]
array([u'10pm', u'1qh336innfl5', u'33', u'93740', u'
                                          '],
        dtype='<U79')
```

Now, are these the examples in the first document? Let's check that using the following command:

```
>>> '10pm' in newgroups.data[0].lower()
True
>>> '1qh336innfl5' in newgroups.data[0].lower()
True
```

## How to do it...

Ok, so it took a bit longer than normal to get the data ready, but we're dealing with text data that isn't as quickly represented as a matrix as the data we're used to.

However, now that we're ready, we'll fire up the classifier and fit our model:

```
>>> from sklearn import naive_bayes
>>> clf = naive_bayes.GaussianNB()
```

Before we fit the model, let's split the dataset into a training and test set:

```
>>> mask = np.random.choice([True, False], len(bow))
>>> clf.fit(bow[mask], newgroups.target[mask])
>>> predictions = clf.predict(bow[~mask])
```

Now that we fit a model on a test set, and then predicted the training set in an attempt to determine which categories go with which articles, let's get a sense of the approximate accuracy:

```
>>> np.mean(predictions == newgroups.target[~mask])

0.92446043165467628
```

## How it works...

The fundamental idea of how Naïve Bayes works is that we can estimate the probability of some data point being a class, given the feature vector.

This can be rearranged via the Bayes formula to give the MAP estimate for the feature vector. This MAP estimate chooses the class for which the feature vector's probability is maximized.

## There's more...

We can also extend Naïve Bayes to do multiclass work. Instead of assuming a Gaussian likelihood, we'll use a multinomial likelihood.

First, let's get a third category of data:

```
>>> from sklearn.datasets import fetch_20newsgroups
>>> mn_categories = ["rec.autos", "rec.motorcycles",
                     "talk.politics.guns"]
>>> mn_newgroups = fetch_20newsgroups(categories=mn_categories)
```

We'll need to vectorize this just like the class case:

```
>>> mn_bow = count_vec.fit_transform(mn_newgroups.data)
>>> mn_bow = np.array(mn_bow.todense())
```

Let's create a mask array to train and test:

```
>>> mn_mask = np.random.choice([True, False], len(mn_newgroups.data))
>>> multinom = naive_bayes.MultinomialNB()
>>> multinom.fit(mn_bow[mn_mask], mn_newgroups.target[mn_mask])

>>> mn_predict = multinom.predict(mn_bow[~mn_mask])
>>> np.mean(mn_predict == mn_newgroups.target[~mn_mask])
0.96594778660612934
```

It's not completely surprising that we did well. We did fairly well in the dual class case, and since one will guess that the `talk.politics.guns` category is fairly orthogonal to the other two, we should probably do pretty well.

# Label propagation with semi-supervised learning

Label propagation is a **semi-supervised** technique that makes use of the labeled and unlabeled data to learn about the unlabeled data. Quite often, data that will benefit from a classification algorithm is difficult to label. For example, labeling data might be very expensive, so only a subset is cost-effective to manually label. This said, there does seem to be slow, but growing, support for companies to hire taxonomists.

## Getting ready

Another problem area is censored data. You can imagine a case where the frontier of time will affect your ability to gather labeled data. Say, for instance, you took measurements of patients and gave them an experimental drug. In some cases, you are able to measure the outcome of the drug, if it happens fast enough, but you might want to predict the outcome of the drugs that have a slower reaction time. The drug might cause a fatal reaction for some patients, and life-saving measures might need to be taken.

## How to do it...

In order to represent the semi-supervised or censored data, we'll need to do a little data preprocessing. First, we'll walk through a simple example, and then we'll move on to some more difficult cases:

```
>>> from sklearn import datasets
>>> d = datasets.load_iris()
```

Due to the fact that we'll be messing with the data, let's make copies and add an unlabeled member to the target name's copy. It'll make it easier to identify data later:

```
>>> X = d.data.copy()
>>> y = d.target.copy()
>>> names = d.target_names.copy()

>>> names = np.append(names, ['unlabeled'])
>>> names
array(['setosa', 'versicolor', 'virginica', 'unlabeled'],
      dtype='|S10')
```

Now, let's update y with -1. This is the marker for the unlabeled case. This is also why we added unlabeled to the end of names:

```
>>> y[np.random.choice([True, False], len(y))] = -1
```

Our data now has a bunch of negative ones (-1) interspersed with the actual data:

```
>>> y[:10]
array([-1, -1, -1, -1,  0,  0, -1, -1,  0, -1])

>>> names[y[:10]]
array(['unlabeled', 'unlabeled', 'unlabeled', 'unlabeled', 'setosa',
       'setosa', 'unlabeled', 'unlabeled', 'setosa', 'unlabeled'],
      dtype='|S10')
```

We clearly have a lot of unlabeled data, and the goal now is to use LabelPropagation to predict the labels:

```
>>> from sklearn import semi_supervised
>>> lp = semi_supervised.LabelPropagation()

>>> lp.fit(X, y)

LabelPropagation(alpha=1, gamma=20, kernel='rbf', max_iter=30,
                 n_neighbors=7, tol=0.001)
```

```
>>> preds = lp.predict(X)
>>> (preds == d.target).mean()
0.98666666666666669
```

Not too bad, though we did use all the data, so it's kind of cheating. Also, the `iris` dataset is a fairly separated dataset.

While we're at it, let's look at `LabelSpreading`, the "sister" class of `LabelPropagation`. We'll make the technical distinction between `LabelPropagation` and `LabelSpreading` in the *How it works...* section of this recipe, but it's easy to say that they are extremely similar:

```
>>> ls = semi_supervised.LabelSpreading()
```

`LabelSpreading` is more robust and noisy as observed from the way it works:

```
>>> ls.fit(X, y)
LabelSpreading(alpha=0.2, gamma=20, kernel='rbf', max_iter=30,
               n_neighbors=7, tol=0.001)
```

```
>>> (ls.predict(X) == d.target).mean()
0.96666666666666667
```

Don't consider the fact that the label-spreading algorithm missed one more as an indication and that it performs worse in general. The whole point is that we might give some ability to predict well on the training set and to work on a wider range of situations.

## How it works...

Label propagation works by creating a graph of the data points, with weights placed on the edge equal to the following:

$$w_{ij}(\theta) = \frac{d_{ij}}{\theta^2}$$

The algorithm then works by labeled data points propagating their labels to the unlabeled data. This propagation is in part determined by edge weight.

The edge weights can be placed in a matrix of transition probabilities. We can iteratively determine a good estimate of the actual labels.

# 5
# Postmodel Workflow

This chapter will cover the following recipes:

- ▸ K-fold cross validation
- ▸ Automatic cross validation
- ▸ Cross validation with ShuffleSplit
- ▸ Stratified k-fold
- ▸ Poor man's grid search
- ▸ Brute force grid search
- ▸ Using dummy estimators to compare results
- ▸ Regression model evaluation
- ▸ Feature selection
- ▸ Feature selection on L1 norms
- ▸ Persisting models with joblib

## Introduction

Even though by design the chapters are unordered, you could argue by virtue of the art of data science, we've saved the best for last.

For the most part, each recipe within this chapter is applicable to the various models we've worked with. In some ways, you can think about this chapter as tuning the parameters and features. Ultimately, we need to choose some criteria to determine the "best" model. We'll use various measures to define best. This is covered in the *Regression model evaluation* recipe. Then in the *Cross validation with ShuffleSplit* recipe, we will randomize the evaluation across subsets of the data to help avoid overfitting.

# cross validation

we'll create, quite possibly, the most important post-model validation
ss validation. We'll talk about k-fold cross validation in this recipe. There are
ies of cross validation, each with slightly different randomization schemes.
K-fold is perhaps one of the most well-known randomization schemes.

## Getting ready

We'll create some data and then fit a classifier on the different folds. It's probably worth
mentioning that if you can keep a holdout set, then that would be best. For example, we
have a dataset where $N = 1000$. If we hold out 200 data points, then use cross validation
between the other 800 points to determine the best parameters.

## How to do it...

First, we'll create some fake data, then we'll examine the parameters, and finally, we'll look
at the size of the resulting dataset:

```
>>> N = 1000
>>> holdout = 200

>>> from sklearn.datasets import make_regression
>>> X, y = make_regression(1000, shuffle=True)
```

Now that we have the data, let's hold out 200 points, and then go through the fold scheme
like we normally would:

```
>>> X_h, y_h = X[:holdout], y[:holdout]
>>> X_t, y_t = X[holdout:], y[holdout:]

>>> from sklearn.cross_validation import KFold
```

K-fold gives us the option of choosing how many folds we want, if we want the values to be
indices or Booleans, if want to shuffle the dataset, and finally, the random state (this is mainly
for reproducibility). Indices will actually be removed in later versions. It's assumed to be `True`.

Let's create the cross validation object:

```
>>> kfold = KFold(len(y_t), n_folds=4)
```

Now, we can iterate through the k-fold object:

```
>>> output_string = "Fold: {}, N_train: {}, N_test: {}"

>>> for i, (train, test) in enumerate(kfold):
```

```
    print output_string.format(i, len(y_t[train]), len(y_t[test]))
```

```
Fold: 0, N_train: 600, N_test: 200
Fold: 1, N_train: 600, N_test: 200
Fold: 2, N_train: 600, N_test: 200
Fold: 3, N_train: 600, N_test: 200
```

Each iteration should return the same split size.

## How it works...

It's probably clear, but k-fold works by iterating through the folds and holds out $1/n\_folds *$ N, where N for us was `len(y_t)`.

From a Python perspective, the cross validation objects have an iterator that can be accessed by using the `in` operator. Often times, it's useful to write a wrapper around a cross validation object that will iterate a subset of the data. For example, we may have a dataset that has repeated measures for data points or we may have a dataset with patients and each patient having measures.

We're going to mix it up and use pandas for this part:

```
>>> import numpy as np
>>> import pandas as pd

>>> patients = np.repeat(np.arange(0, 100, dtype=np.int8), 8)

>>> measurements = pd.DataFrame({'patient_id': patients,
                    'ys': np.random.normal(0, 1, 800)})
```

Now that we have the data, we only want to hold out certain customers instead of data points:

```
>>> custids = np.unique(measurements.patient_id)
>>> customer_kfold = KFold(custids.size, n_folds=4)

>>> output_string = "Fold: {}, N_train: {}, N_test: {}"

>>> for i, (train, test) in enumerate(customer_kfold):
        train_cust_ids = custids[train]
        training = measurements[measurements.patient_id.isin(
                train_cust_ids)]
        testing = measurements[~measurements.patient_id.isin(
                train_cust_ids)]
```

```
        print output_string.format(i, len(training), len(testing))
```

```
Fold: 0, N_train: 600, N_test: 200
Fold: 1, N_train: 600, N_test: 200
Fold: 2, N_train: 600, N_test: 200
Fold: 3, N_train: 600, N_test: 200
```

# Automatic cross validation

We've looked at the using cross validation iterators that scikit-learn comes with, but we can also use a helper function to perform cross validation for use automatically. This is similar to how other objects in scikit-learn are wrapped by helper functions, pipeline for instance.

## Getting ready

First, we'll need to create a sample classifier; this can really be anything, a decision tree, a random forest, whatever. For us, it'll be a random forest. We'll then create a dataset and use the cross validation functions.

## How to do it...

First import the `ensemble` module and we'll get started:

```
>>> from sklearn import ensemble
>>> rf = ensemble.RandomForestRegressor(max_features='auto')
```

Okay, so now, let's create some regression data:

```
>>> from sklearn import datasets
>>> X, y = datasets.make_regression(10000, 10)
```

Now that we have the data, we can import the `cross_validation` module and get access to the functions we'll use:

```
>>> from sklearn import cross_validation
```

```
>>> scores = cross_validation.cross_val_score(rf, X, y)
```

```
>>> print scores
```

```
[ 0.86823874  0.86763225  0.86986129]
```

## How it works...

For the most part, this will delegate to the cross validation objects. One nice thing is that, the function will handle performing the cross validation in parallel.

We can activate verbose mode play by play:

```
>>> scores = cross_validation.cross_val_score(rf, X, y, verbose=3,
        cv=4)

[CV]  no parameters to be set
[CV]  no parameters to be set, score=0.872866 -    0.7s
[CV]  no parameters to be set
[CV]  no parameters to be set, score=0.873679 -    0.6s
[CV]  no parameters to be set
[CV]  no parameters to be set, score=0.878018 -    0.7s
[CV]  no parameters to be set
[CV]  no parameters to be set, score=0.871598 -    0.6s

[Parallel(n_jobs=1)]: Done    1 jobs      | elapsed:    0.7s
[Parallel(n_jobs=1)]: Done    4 out of    4 | elapsed:    2.6s finished
```

As we can see, during each iteration, we scored the function. We also get an idea of how long the model runs.

It's also worth knowing that we can score our function predicated on which kind of model we're trying to fit. In other recipes, we've discussed how to create your own scoring function.

# Cross validation with ShuffleSplit

ShuffleSplit is one of the simplest cross validation techniques. This cross validation technique will simply take a sample of the data for the number of iterations specified.

## Getting ready

ShuffleSplit is another cross validation technique that is very simple. We'll specify the total elements in the dataset, and it will take care of the rest. We'll walk through an example of estimating the mean of a univariate dataset. This is somewhat similar to resampling, but it'll illustrate one reason why we want to use cross validation while showing cross validation.

## How to do it...

First, we need to create the dataset. We'll use NumPy to create a dataset, where we know the underlying mean. We'll sample half of the dataset to estimate the mean and see how close it is to the underlying mean:

```
>>> import numpy as np

>>> true_loc = 1000
>>> true_scale = 10
>>> N = 1000

>>> dataset = np.random.normal(true_loc, true_scale, N)


>>> import matplotlib.pyplot as plt

>>> f, ax = plt.subplots(figsize=(7, 5))

>>> ax.hist(dataset, color='k', alpha=.65, histtype='stepfilled');
>>> ax.set_title("Histogram of dataset");

>>> f.savefig("978-1-78398-948-5_06_06.png")
```

NumPy will give the following output:

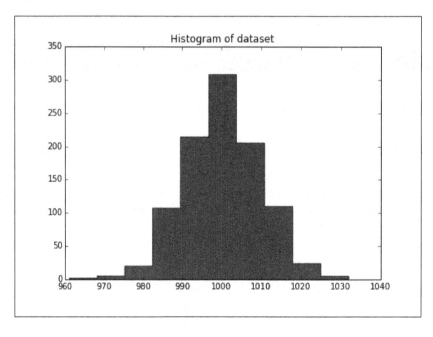

Now, let's take the first half of the data and guess the mean:

```
>>> from sklearn import cross_validation

>>> holdout_set = dataset[:500]
>>> fitting_set = dataset[500:]

>>> estimate = fitting_set[:N/2].mean()

>>> import matplotlib.pyplot as plt

>>> f, ax = plt.subplots(figsize=(7, 5))

>>> ax.set_title("True Mean vs Regular Estimate")

>>> ax.vlines(true_loc, 0, 1, color='r', linestyles='-', lw=5,
              alpha=.65, label='true mean')
>>> ax.vlines(estimate, 0, 1, color='g', linestyles='-', lw=5,
              alpha=.65, label='regular estimate')

>>> ax.set_xlim(999, 1001)

>>> ax.legend()

>>> f.savefig("978-1-78398-948-5_06_07.png")
```

We'll get the following output:

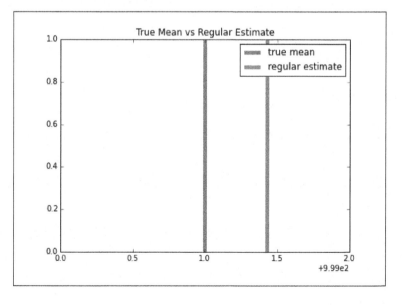

Now, we can use ShuffleSplit to fit the estimator on several smaller datasets:

```
>>> from sklearn.cross_validation import ShuffleSplit


>>> shuffle_split = ShuffleSplit(len(fitting_set))


>>> mean_p = []

>>> for train, _ in shuffle_split:
        mean_p.append(fitting_set[train].mean())
        shuf_estimate = np.mean(mean_p)


>>> import matplotlib.pyplot as plt

>>> f, ax = plt.subplots(figsize=(7, 5))

>>> ax.vlines(true_loc, 0, 1, color='r', linestyles='-', lw=5,
              alpha=.65, label='true mean')
>>> ax.vlines(estimate, 0, 1, color='g', linestyles='-', lw=5,
              alpha=.65, label='regular estimate')
>>> ax.vlines(shuf_estimate, 0, 1, color='b', linestyles='-', lw=5,
              alpha=.65, label='shufflesplit estimate')

>>> ax.set_title("All Estimates")
>>> ax.set_xlim(999, 1001)

>>> ax.legend(loc=3)
```

The output will be as follows:

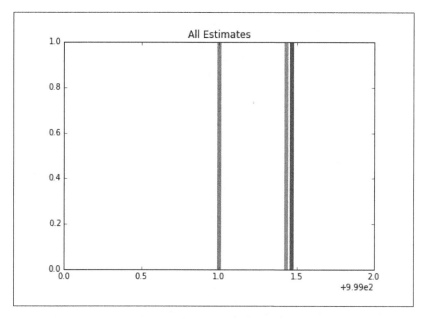

As we can see, we got an estimate that was similar to what we expected, but we were able to take many samples to get that estimate.

# Stratified k-fold

In this recipe, we'll quickly look at stratified k-fold valuation. We've walked through different recipes where the class representation was unbalanced in some manner. Stratified k-fold is nice because its scheme is specifically designed to maintain the class proportions.

## Getting ready

We're going to create a small dataset. In this dataset, we will then use stratified k-fold validation. We want it small so that we can see the variation. For larger samples. it probably won't be as big of a deal.

We'll then plot the class proportions at each step to illustrate how the class proportions are maintained:

```
>>> from sklearn import datasets
>>> X, y = datasets.make_classification(n_samples=int(1e3),
         weights=[1./11])
```

Let's check the overall class weight distribution:

```
>>> y.mean()
```

0.90300000000000002

Roughly, 90.5 percent of the samples are 1, with the balance 0.

## How to do it...

Let's create a stratified k-fold object and iterate it through each fold. We'll measure the proportion of `verse` that are 1. After that we'll plot the proportion of classes by the split number to see how and if it changes. This code will hopefully illustrate how this is beneficial. We'll also plot this code against a basic ShuffleSplit:

```
>>> from sklearn import cross_validation

>>> n_folds = 50

>>> strat_kfold = cross_validation.StratifiedKFold(y,
                    n_folds=n_folds)
>>> shuff_split = cross_validation.ShuffleSplit(n=len(y),
                    n_iter=n_folds)

>>> kfold_y_props = []
>>> shuff_y_props = []

>>> for (k_train, k_test), (s_train, s_test) in zip(strat_kfold,
>>> shuff_split):
        kfold_y_props.append(y[k_train].mean())
        shuff_y_props.append(y[s_train].mean())
```

Now, let's plot the proportions over each fold:

```
>>> import matplotlib.pyplot as plt

>>> f, ax = plt.subplots(figsize=(7, 5))

>>> ax.plot(range(n_folds), shuff_y_props, label="ShuffleSplit",
            color='k')
>>> ax.plot(range(n_folds), kfold_y_props, label="Stratified",
            color='k', ls='--')
>>> ax.set_title("Comparing class proportions.")

>>> ax.legend(loc='best')
```

The output will be as follows:

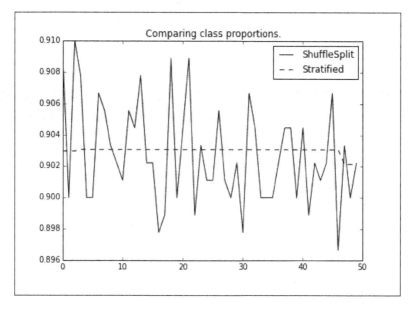

We can see that the proportion of each fold for stratified k-fold is stable across folds.

## How it works...

Stratified k-fold works by taking the $y$ value. First, getting the overall proportion of the classes, then intelligently splitting the training and test set into the proportions. This will generalize to multiple labels:

```
>>> import numpy as np

>>> three_classes = np.random.choice([1,2,3], p=[.1, .4, .5],
                    size=1000)

>>> import itertools as it

>>> for train, test in cross_validation.StratifiedKFold(three_classes, 5):
        print np.bincount(three_classes[train])

[   0   90  314  395]
[   0   90  314  395]
```

```
[   0   90  314  395]
[   0   91  315  395]
[   0   91  315  396]
```

As we can see, we got roughly the sample sizes of each class for our training and testing proportions.

# Poor man's grid search

In this recipe, we're going to introduce grid search with basic Python, though we will use sklearn for the models and matplotlib for the visualization.

## Getting ready

In this recipe, we will perform the following tasks:

- Design a basic search grid in the parameter space
- Iterate through the grid and check the loss/score function at each point in the parameter space for the dataset
- Choose the point in the parameter space that minimizes/maximizes the evaluation function

Also, the model we'll fit is a basic decision tree classifier. Our parameter space will be 2 dimensional to help us with the visualization:

$$criteria = \{gini, entropy\}$$

$$max\_features = \{auto, log2, None\}$$

The parameter space will then be the Cartesian product of the those two sets:

$$parameter\ space = criteria \times max\_features$$

We'll see in a bit how we can iterate through this space with itertools.

Let's create the dataset and then get started:

```
>>> from sklearn import datasets
>>> X, y = datasets.make_classification(n_samples=2000, n_features=10)
```

## How to do it...

Earlier we said that we'd use grid search to tune two parameters—`criteria` and `max_features`. We need to represent those as Python sets, and then use `itertools` product to iterate through them:

```
>>> criteria = {'gini', 'entropy'}
>>> max_features = {'auto', 'log2', None}
>>> import itertools as it
>>> parameter_space = it.product(criteria, max_features)
```

Great! So now that we have the parameter space, let's iterate through it and check the accuracy of each model as specified by the parameters. Then, we'll store that accuracy so that we can compare different parameter spaces. We'll also use a test and train split of 50, 50:

```
import numpy as np
train_set = np.random.choice([True, False], size=len(y))
from sklearn.tree import DecisionTreeClassifier
accuracies = {}
for criterion, max_feature in parameter_space:
    dt = DecisionTreeClassifier(criterion=criterion,
        max_features=max_feature)
    dt.fit(X[train_set], y[train_set])
    accuracies[(criterion, max_feature)] = (dt.predict(X[~train_set])
                                      == y[~train_set]).mean()
>>> accuracies
{('entropy', None): 0.974609375, ('entropy', 'auto'): 0.9736328125,
('entropy', 'log2'): 0.962890625, ('gini', None): 0.9677734375, ('gini',
'auto'): 0.9638671875, ('gini', 'log2'): 0.96875}
```

So we now have the accuracies and its performance. Let's visualize the performance:

```
>>> from matplotlib import pyplot as plt
>>> from matplotlib import cm
>>> cmap = cm.RdBu_r
>>> f, ax = plt.subplots(figsize=(7, 4))
>>> ax.set_xticklabels([''] + list(criteria))
>>> ax.set_yticklabels([''] + list(max_features))
>>> plot_array = []
>>> for max_feature in max_features:
```

```
    m = []
>>> for criterion in criteria:
        m.append(accuracies[(criterion, max_feature)])
        plot_array.append(m)
>>> colors = ax.matshow(plot_array, vmin=np.min(accuracies.values()) -
            0.001, vmax=np.max(accuracies.values()) + 0.001, cmap=cmap)
>>> f.colorbar(colors)
```

The following is the output:

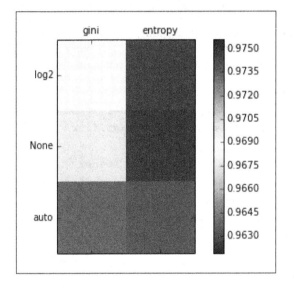

It's fairly easy to see which one performed best here. Hopefully, you can see how this process can be taken to the further stage with a brute force method.

## How it works...

This works fairly simply, we just have to perform the following steps:

1. Choose a set of parameters.
2. Iterate through them and find the accuracy of each step.
3. Find the best performer by visual inspection.

# Brute force grid search

In this recipe, we'll do an exhaustive grid search through scikit-learn. This is basically the same thing we did in the previous recipe, but we'll utilize built-in methods.

We'll also walk through an example of performing randomized optimization. This is an alternative to brute force search. Essentially, we're trading computer cycles to make sure that we search the entire space. We were fairly calm in the last recipe. However, you could imagine a model that has several steps, first imputation for fix missing data, then PCA reduce the dimensionality to classification. Your parameter space could get very large, very fast; therefore, it can be advantageous to only search a part of that space.

## Getting ready

To get started, we'll need to perform the following steps:

1. Create some classification data.
2. We'll then create a `LogisticRegression` object that will be the model we're fitting.
3. After that, we'll create the search objects, `GridSearch` and `RandomizedSearchCV`.

## How to do it...

Run the following code to create some classification data:

```
>>> from sklearn.datasets import make_classification

>>> X, y = make_classification(1000, n_features=5)
```

Now, we'll create our logistic regression object:

```
>>> from sklearn.linear_model import LogisticRegression

>>> lr = LogisticRegression(class_weight='auto')
```

We need to specify the parameters we want to search. For `GridSearch`, we can just specify the ranges that we care about, but for `RandomizedSearchCV`, we'll need to actually specify the distribution over the same space from which to sample:

```
>>> lr.fit(X, y)

LogisticRegression(C=1.0, class_weight={0: 0.25, 1: 0.75}, dual=False,
                  fit_intercept=True, intercept_scaling=1,
                  penalty='12', random_state=None, tol=0.0001)
```

```
>>> grid_search_params = {'penalty': ['l1', 'l2'],
                          'C': [1, 2, 3, 4]}
```

The only change we'll need to make is to describe the C parameter as a probability distribution. We'll keep it simple right now, though we will use `scipy` to describe the distribution:

```
>>> import scipy.stats as st
>>> import numpy as np
```

```
>>> random_search_params = {'penalty': ['l1', 'l2'],
                            'C': st.randint(1, 4)}
```

## How it works...

Now, we'll fit the classifier. This works by passing `lr` to the parameter search objects:

```
>>> from sklearn.grid_search import GridSearchCV, RandomizedSearchCV
```

```
>>> gs = GridSearchCV(lr, grid_search_params)
```

`GridSearchCV` implements the same API as the other models:

```
>>> gs.fit(X, y)
```

```
GridSearchCV(cv=None, estimator=LogisticRegression(C=1.0,
             class_weight='auto', dual=False, fit_intercept=True,
             intercept_scaling=1, penalty='l2', random_state=None,
             tol=0.0001), fit_params={}, iid=True, loss_func=None,
             n_jobs=1, param_grid={'penalty': ['l1', 'l2'],
             'C': [1, 2, 3, 4]}, pre_dispatch='2*n_jobs', refit=True,
             score_func=None, scoring=None, verbose=0)
```

As we can see with the `param_grid` parameter, our `penalty` and C are both arrays.

To access the scores, we can use the `grid_scores_` attribute of the grid search. We also want to find the optimal set of parameters. We can also look at the marginal performance of the grid search:

```
>>> gs.grid_scores_

[mean: 0.90300, std: 0.01192, params: {'penalty': 'l1', 'C': 1},
 mean: 0.90100, std: 0.01258, params: {'penalty': 'l2', 'C': 1},
 mean: 0.90200, std: 0.01117, params: {'penalty': 'l1', 'C': 2},
 mean: 0.90100, std: 0.01258, params: {'penalty': 'l2', 'C': 2},
 mean: 0.90200, std: 0.01117, params: {'penalty': 'l1', 'C': 3},
 mean: 0.90100, std: 0.01258, params: {'penalty': 'l2', 'C': 3},
 mean: 0.90100, std: 0.01258, params: {'penalty': 'l1', 'C': 4},
 mean: 0.90100, std: 0.01258, params: {'penalty': 'l2', 'C': 4}]
```

We might want to get the max score:

```
>>> gs.grid_scores_[1][1]

0.90100000000000002

>>> max(gs.grid_scores_, key=lambda x: x[1])

mean: 0.90300, std: 0.01192, params: {'penalty': 'l1', 'C': 1}
```

The parameters obtained are the best choices for our logistic regression.

# Using dummy estimators to compare results

This recipe is about creating fake estimators; this isn't the pretty or exciting stuff, but it is worthwhile to have a reference point for the model you'll eventually build.

## Getting ready

In this recipe, we'll perform the following tasks:

1. Create some data random data.
2. Fit the various dummy estimators.

We'll perform these two steps for regression data and classification data.

## How to do it...

First, we'll create the random data:

```
>>> from sklearn.datasets import make_regression, make_classification
# classification if for later

>>> X, y = make_regression()

>>> from sklearn import dummy

>>> dumdum = dummy.DummyRegressor()

>>> dumdum.fit(X, y)

DummyRegressor(constant=None, strategy='mean')
```

By default, the estimator will predict by just taking the mean of the values and predicting the mean values:

```
>>> dumdum.predict(X)[:5]

array([ 2.23297907,  2.23297907,  2.23297907,  2.23297907,
        2.23297907])
```

There are other two other strategies we can try. We can predict a supplied constant (refer to `constant=None` from the preceding command). We can also predict the median value.

Supplying a constant will only be considered if strategy is "constant".

Let's have a look:

```
>>> predictors = [("mean", None),
                  ("median", None),
                  ("constant", 10)]

>>> for strategy, constant in predictors:
        dumdum = dummy.DummyRegressor(strategy=strategy,
                constant=constant)
>>> dumdum.fit(X, y)

>>> print "strategy: {}".format(strategy), ",".join(map(str,
        dumdum.predict(X)[:5]))

 strategy: mean 2.23297906733,2.23297906733,2.23297906733,2.23297906733,2
.23297906733
```

```
strategy: median 20.38535248,20.38535248,20.38535248,20.38535248,20.38535
248
strategy: constant 10.0,10.0,10.0,10.0,10.0
```

We actually have four options for classifiers. These strategies are similar to the continuous case, it's just slanted toward classification problems:

```
>>> predictors = [("constant", 0),
                  ("stratified", None),
                  ("uniform", None),
                  ("most_frequent", None)]
```

We'll also need to create some classification data:

```
>>> X, y = make_classification()
```

```
>>> for strategy, constant in predictors:
        dumdum = dummy.DummyClassifier(strategy=strategy,
            constant=constant)
        dumdum.fit(X, y)
        print "strategy: {}".format(strategy), ",".join(map(str,
            dumdum.predict(X)[:5]))
```

```
strategy: constant 0,0,0,0,0
strategy: stratified 1,0,0,1,0
strategy: uniform 0,0,0,1,1
strategy: most_frequent 1,1,1,1,1
```

## How it works...

It's always good to test your models against the simplest models and that's exactly what the dummy estimators give you. For example, imagine a fraud model. In this model, only 5 percent of the data set is fraud. Therefore, we can probably fit a pretty good model just by never guessing any fraud.

We can create this model by using the stratified strategy, using the following command. We can also get a good example of why class imbalance causes problems:

```
>>> X, y = make_classification(20000, weights=[.95, .05])
```

```
>>> dumdum = dummy.DummyClassifier(strategy='most_frequent')
```

```
>>> dumdum.fit(X, y)
```

```
DummyClassifier(constant=None, random_state=None, strategy='most_
frequent')

>>> from sklearn.metrics import accuracy_score

>>> print accuracy_score(y, dumdum.predict(X))

0.94575
```

We were actually correct very often, but that's not the point. The point is that this is our baseline. If we cannot create a model for fraud that is more accurate than this, then it isn't worth our time.

# Regression model evaluation

We learned about quantifying the error in classification, now we'll discuss quantifying the error for continuous problems. For example, we're trying to predict an age, not a gender.

## Getting ready

Like the classification, we'll fake some data, then plot the change. We'll start simple, then build up the complexity. The data will be a simulated linear model:

```
m = 2
b = 1

y = lambda x: m*x+b
```

Also, let's get our modules loaded:

```
>>> import numpy as np
>>> import matplotlib.pyplot as plt
>>> from sklearn import metrics
```

## How to do it...

We will be performing the following actions:

1. Use 'y' to generate 'y_actual'.
2. Use 'y_actual' plus some err to generate 'y_prediction'.
3. Plot the differences.
4. Walk through various metrics and plot some of them.

Let's take care of steps 1 and 2 at the same time and just have a function do the work for us. This will be almost the same thing we just saw, but we'll add the ability to specify an error (or bias if a constant):

```
>>> def data(x, m=2, b=1, e=None, s=10):
        """
        Args:
            x: The x value
            m: Slope
            b: Intercept
            e: Error, optional, True will give random error
        """

        if e is None:
            e_i = 0
        elif e is True:
            e_i = np.random.normal(0, s, len(xs))
        else:
            e_i = e

        return x * m + b + e_i
```

Now that we have the function, let's define `y_hat` and `y_actual`. We'll do it in a convenient way:

```
>>> from functools import partial

>>> N = 100
>>> xs = np.sort(np.random.rand(N)*100)

>>> y_pred_gen = partial(data, x=xs, e=True)
>>> y_true_gen = partial(data, x=xs)

>>> y_pred = y_pred_gen()
>>> y_true = y_true_gen()


>>> f, ax = plt.subplots(figsize=(7, 5))

>>> ax.set_title("Plotting the fit vs the underlying process.")
>>> ax.scatter(xs, y_pred, label=r'$\hat{y}$')
```

```
>>> ax.plot(xs, y_true, label=r'$y$')
```

```
>>> ax.legend(loc='best')
```

The output for this code is as follows:

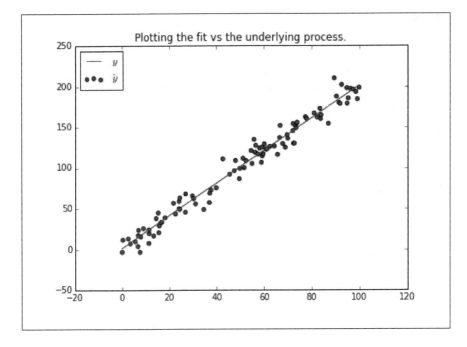

Just to confirm the output, we'd be working with the classical residuals:

```
>>> e_hat = y_pred - y_true
```

```
>>> f, ax = plt.subplots(figsize=(7, 5))
```

```
>>> ax.set_title("Residuals")
>>> ax.hist(e_hat, color='r', alpha=.5, histtype='stepfilled')
```

The output for the residuals is as follows:

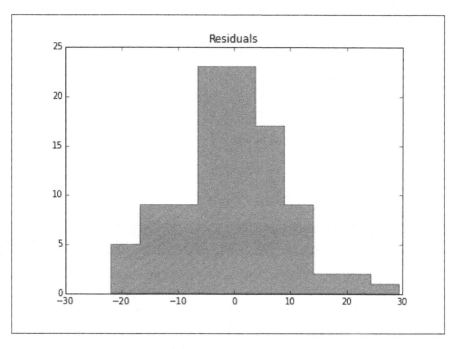

So that looks good now.

## How it works...

Now let's move to the metrics.

First, a metric is the mean squared error:

$$MSE\left(y_{trus}, y_{pred}\right) = E\left(\left(y_{trus} - y_{pred}\right)^2\right)$$

You can use the following code to find the value of the mean squared error:

```
>>> metrics.mean_squared_error(y_true, y_pred)
```

```
93.342352628475368
```

You'll notice that this code will penalize large errors more than small errors. It's important to remember that all we're doing here is applying what probably was the cost function for the model on the test data.

Another option is the mean absolute deviation. We need to take the absolute value of the difference, if we don't, our value will probably be fairly close to zero, the mean of the distribution:

$$MAD\left(y_{trus}, y_{pred}\right) = E\left(\mid y_{trus} - y_{pred}\mid\right)$$

The final option is $R^2$, this is 1 minus the ratio of squared errors for the overall mean and the fit model. As the ratio tends to 0, the $R^2$ tends to 1:

```
>>> metrics.r2_score(y_true, y_pred)
```

```
0.9729312117010761
```

$R^2$ is deceptive; it cannot give the clearest sense of the accuracy of the model.

# Feature selection

This recipe along with the two following it will be centered around automatic feature selection. I like to think of this as the feature analogue of parameter tuning. In the same way that we cross-validate to find an appropriately general parameter, we can find an appropriately general subset of features. This will involve several different methods.

The simplest idea is univariate selection. The other methods involve working with a combination of features.

An added benefit to feature selection is that it can ease the burden on the data collection. Imagine that you have built a model on a very small subset of the data. If all goes well, you might want to scale up to predict the model on the entire subset of data. If this is the case, you can ease the engineering effort of data collection at that scale.

## Getting ready

With univariate feature selection, scoring functions will come to the forefront again. This time, they will define the comparable measure by which we can eliminate features.

In this recipe, we'll fit a regression model with a few 10,000 features, but only 1,000 points. We'll walk through the various univariate feature selection methods:

```
>>> from sklearn import datasets
>>> X, y = datasets.make_regression(1000, 10000)
```

Now that we have the data, we will compare the features that are included with the various methods. This is actually a very common situation when you're dealing in text analysis or some areas of bioinformatics.

## How to do it...

First, we need to import the `feature_selection` module:

```
>>> from sklearn import feature_selection
>>> f, p = feature_selection.f_regression(X, y)
```

Here, `f` is the f score associated with each linear model fit with just one of the features. We can then compare these features and based on this comparison, we can cull features. `p` is also the *p* value associated with that *f* value.

In statistics, the `p` value is the probability of a value more extreme than the current value of the test statistic. Here, the `f` value is the test statistic:

```
>>> f[:5]
array([  1.06271357e-03,  2.91136869e+00,  1.01886922e+00,
         2.22483130e+00,  4.67624756e-01])
>>> p[:5]
array([ 0.97400066,  0.08826831,  0.31303204,  0.1361235,  0.49424067])
```

As we can see, many of the p values are quite large. We would rather want that the p values be quite small. So, we can grab NumPy out of our tool box and choose all the p values less than .05. These will be the features we'll use for the analysis:

```
>>> import numpy as np
>>> idx = np.arange(0, X.shape[1])
>>> features_to_keep = idx[p < .05]
>>> len(features_to_keep)
```

```
501
```

As you can see, we're actually keeping a relatively large amount of features. Depending on the context of the model, we can tighten this p value. This will lessen the number of features kept.

Another option is using the `VarianceThreshold` object. We've learned a bit about it, but it's important to understand that our ability to fit models is largely based on the variance created by features. If there is no variance, then our features cannot describe the variation in the dependent variable. A nice feature of this, as per the documentation, is that because it does not use the outcome variable, it can be used for unsupervised cases.

We will need to set the threshold for which we eliminate features. In order to do that, we just take the median of the feature variances and supply that:

```
>>> var_threshold = feature_selection.VarianceThreshold(np.median(np.
                   var(X, axis=1)))
```

```
>>> var_threshold.fit_transform(X).shape
```

```
(1000, 4835)
```

As we can see, we eliminated roughly half the features, more or less what we would expect.

## How it works...

In general, all these methods work by fitting a basic model with a single feature. Depending on whether we have a classification problem or a regression problem, we can use the appropriate scoring function.

Let's look at a smaller problem and visualize how feature selection will eliminate certain features. We'll use the same scoring function from the first example, but just 20 features:

```
>>> X, y = datasets.make_regression(10000, 20)
```

```
>>> f, p = feature_selection.f_regression(X, y)
```

Now let's plot the p values of the features, we can see which feature will be eliminated and which will be kept:

```
>>> from matplotlib import pyplot as plt
```

```
>>> f, ax = plt.subplots(figsize=(7, 5))
```

```
>>> ax.bar(np.arange(20), p, color='k')
>>> ax.set_title("Feature p values")
```

The output will be as follows:

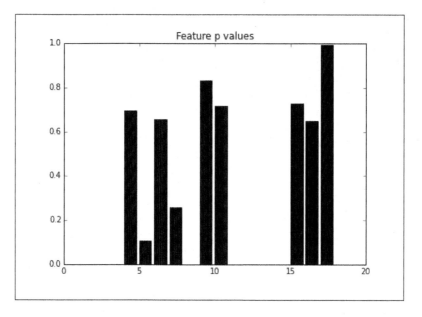

As we can see, many of the features won't be kept, but several will be.

# Feature selection on L1 norms

We're going to work with some ideas similar to those we saw in the recipe on Lasso Regression. In that recipe, we looked at the number of features that had zero coefficients.

Now we're going to take this a step further and use the spareness associated with L1 norms to preprocess the features.

## Getting ready

We'll use the diabetes dataset to fit a regression. First, we'll fit a basic `LinearRegression` model with a `ShuffleSplit` cross validation. After we do that, we'll use `LassoRegression` to find the coefficients that are 0 when using an `L1` penalty. This hopefully will help us to avoid overfitting, which means that the model is too specific to the data it was trained on. To put this another way, the model, if overfit, does not generalize well to outside data.

We're going to perform the following steps:

1. Load the dataset.
2. Fit a basic linear regression model.

3. Use feature selection to remove uninformative features.

4. Refit the linear regression and check to see how well it fits compared with the fully featured model.

## How to do it...

First, let's get the dataset:

```
>>> import sklearn.datasets as ds
>>> diabetes = ds.load_diabetes()
```

Let's create the LinearRegression object:

```
>>> from sklearn import linear_model
>>> lr = linear_model.LinearRegression()
```

Let's also import the metrics module for the mean_squared_error function and the cross_validation module for the ShuffleSplit cross validation scheme:

```
>>> from sklearn import metrics
>>> from sklearn import cross_validation


>>> shuff = cross_validation.ShuffleSplit(diabetes.target.size)
```

Now, let's fit the model, and we'll keep track of the mean squared error for each iteration of ShuffleSplit:

```
>>> mses = []
>>> for train, test in shuff:
        train_X = diabetes.data[train]
        train_y = diabetes.target[train]

        test_X = diabetes.data[~train]
        test_y = diabetes.target[~train]

        lr.fit(train_X, train_y)

        mses.append(metrics.mean_squared_error(test_y,
                 lr.predict(test_X)))

>>> np.mean(mses)

2856.366626198198
```

So now that we have the regular fit, let's check it after we eliminate any features with a zero for the coefficient. Let's fit the Lasso Regression:

```
>>> from sklearn import feature_selection
>>> from sklearn import cross_validation


>>> cv = linear_model.LassoCV()
>>> cv.fit(diabetes.data, diabetes.target)
>>> cv.coef_

array([ -0. , -226.2375274 ,   526.85738059,   314.44026013,
        -196.92164002, 1.48742026, -151.78054083, 106.52846989,
        530.58541123, 64.50588257])
```

We'll remove the first feature, I'll use a NumPy array to represent the columns that are to be included in the model:

```
>>> import numpy as np
>>> columns = np.arange(diabetes.data.shape[1])[cv.coef_ != 0]
>>> columns
array([1, 2, 3 4, 5, 6, 7, 8, 9])
```

Okay, so now we'll fit the model with the specific features (see the columns in the following code block):

```
>>> l1mses = []

>>> for train, test in shuff:
        train_X = diabetes.data[train][:, columns]
        train_y = diabetes.target[train]

        test_X = diabetes.data[~train][:, columns]
        test_y = diabetes.target[~train]

        lr.fit(train_X, train_y)

        l1mses.append(metrics.mean_squared_error(test_y,
                    lr.predict(test_X)))

>>> np.mean(l1mses)
2861.0763924492171
>>> np.mean(l1mses) - np.mean(mses)
4.7097662510191185
```

As we can see, even though we get an uninformative feature, the model still fits worse. This isn't always the case. In the next section, we'll compare a fit between models where there are many uninformative features.

## How it works...

First, we're going to create a regression dataset with many uninformative features:

```
>>> X, y = ds.make_regression(noise=5)
```

Let's fit a normal regression:

```
>>> mses = []
```

```
>>> shuff = cross_validation.ShuffleSplit(y.size)
```

```
>>> for train, test in shuff:
        train_X = X[train]
        train_y = y[train]

        test_X = X[~train]
        test_y = y[~train]

        lr.fit(train_X, train_y)

        mses.append(metrics.mean_squared_error(test_y,
                lr.predict(test_X)))
>>> np.mean(mses)
```

```
879.75447864034209
```

Now, we can walk through the same process for Lasso regression:

```
>>> cv.fit(X, y)
```

```
LassoCV(alphas=None, copy_X=True, cv=None, eps=0.001,
        fit_intercept=True, max_iter=1000, n_alphas=100,
        n_jobs=1, normalize=False, positive=False, precompute='auto',
        tol=0.0001, verbose=False)
```

We'll create the columns again. This is a nice pattern that will allow us to specify the features we want to include:

```
>>> import numpy as np
>>> columns = np.arange(X.shape[1])[cv.coef_ != 0]
>>> columns[:5]
array([11, 15, 17, 20, 21,])
```

```
>>> mses = []
```

```
>>> shuff = cross_validation.ShuffleSplit(y.size)

>>> for train, test in shuff:
        train_X = X[train][:, columns]
        train_y = y[train]

        test_X = X[~train][:, columns]
        test_y = y[~train]

        lr.fit(train_X, train_y)

        mses.append(metrics.mean_squared_error(test_y,
                    lr.predict(test_X)))

>>> np.mean(mses)

15.755403220117708
```

As we can see, we get an extreme improvement in the fit of the model. This just exemplifies that we need to be cognizant that not all the models need to be or should be thrown into the model.

# Persisting models with joblib

In this recipe, we're going to show how you can keep your model around for a later usage. For example, you might want to actually use a model to predict the outcome and automatically make a decision.

## Getting ready

In this recipe, we will perform the following tasks:

1. Fit the model that we will persist.
2. Import joblib and save the model.

## How to do it...

To persist models with joblib, the following code can be used:

```
>>> from sklearn import datasets, tree

>>> X, y = datasets.make_classification()
```

```
>>> dt = tree.DecisionTreeClassifier()
>>> dt.fit(X, y)

DecisionTreeClassifier(compute_importances=None, criterion='gini',
                    max_depth=None, max_features=None,
                    max_leaf_nodes=None, min_density=None,
                    min_samples_leaf=1, min_samples_split=2,
                    random_state=None, splitter='best')

>>> from sklearn.externals import joblib


>>> joblib.dump(dt, "dtree.clf")

['dtree.clf',
 'dtree.clf_01.npy',
 'dtree.clf_02.npy',
 'dtree.clf_03.npy',
 'dtree.clf_04.npy']
```

## How it works...

The preceding code works by saving the state of the object that can be reloaded into a scikit-learn object. It's important to note that the state of model will have varying levels of complexity, given the model type.

For simplicity sake, consider that all we'd need to save is the way to predict the outcome for the given inputs. Well, for regression that would be easy, a little matrix algebra and we're done. However, for models like random forest, where we could have many trees, and those trees could be of various complexity levels, regression is difficult.

## There's more...

We can check the size of decision tree versus random forest:

```
>>> from sklearn import ensemble

>>> rf = ensemble.RandomForestClassifier()
>>> rf.fit(X, y)

RandomForestClassifier(bootstrap=True, compute_importances=None,
                    criterion='gini', max_depth=None,
                    max_features='auto', max_leaf_nodes=None,
                    min_density=None, min_samples_leaf=1,
                    min_samples_split=2, n_estimators=10,
                    n_jobs=1, oob_score=False, random_state=None,
                    verbose=0)
```

I'm going to omit the output, but in total, there we were 52 files outputted on my machine:

```
>>> joblib.dump(rf, "rf.clf")
['rf.clf',
 'rf.clf_01.npy',
 'rf.clf_02.npy',
 'rf.clf_03.npy',
 'rf.clf_04.npy',
 'rf.clf_05.npy',
 'rf.clf_06.npy',…]
```

# Index

precision parameter 150
preprocessing module 13
principal component analysis. *See* **PCA**
probabilistic clustering
    performing, with Gaussian
        Mixture Models 105-111
pydot 125

# Q

Quadratic Discernment Analysis (QDA)
    about 151
    working with 151, 152

# R

radial basis function
    using 143, 144
random forest model
    tuning 134-139
random forests
    using 130-133
recall parameter 150
regression
    about 115
    Gaussian process, using for 44-48
    k-NN, using for 115-118
    Stochastic Gradient Descent (SGD),
        using for 51-53
regression model
    evaluating 180-184
regularization, LARS 72-75
residuals 57
results
    comparing, dummy estimators used 177-180
ridge cross-validation 67
RidgeCV object 67
ridge regression
    parameter, optimizing 66-69
    used, for overcoming linear regression's
        shortfalls 63-66
root-mean-square deviation (RMSE) 104

# S

sample data
    creating, for toy analysis 10-12
    obtaining, from external sources 8-10
scikit-image 99
scikit-learn
    URL 10
semi-supervised technique 157
ShuffleSplit
    about 165
    used, for performing cross
        validation 165-169
silhouette distance 90
sklearn.metrics.pairwise 102
sparse imputations
    handling 15
sparse matrices 17
sparsity
    used, for regularizing models 70, 71
spherical clusters 105
standard normal
    about 13
    data, scaling to 13-15
Stochastic Gradient Descent (SGD)
    using, for classification 153, 154
    using, for regression 51-53
strategies
    missing values, imputing through 22-24
stratified k-fold valuation
    viewing 169-172
support vector classifier (SVC) 140
support vector machines (SVM)
    about 140
    data, classifying with 140-143
support vectors 140

# T

thresholding
    binary features, creating through 16, 17
toy analysis
    sample data, creating for 10-12

## Thank you for buying
# scikit-learn Cookbook

# About Packt Publishing

Packt, pronounced 'packed', published its first book "*Mastering phpMyAdmin for Effective MySQL Management*" in April 2004 and subsequently continued to specialize in publishing highly focused books on specific technologies and solutions.

Our books and publications share the experiences of your fellow IT professionals in adapting and customizing today's systems, applications, and frameworks. Our solution based books give you the knowledge and power to customize the software and technologies you're using to get the job done. Packt books are more specific and less general than the IT books you have seen in the past. Our unique business model allows us to bring you more focused information, giving you more of what you need to know, and less of what you don't.

Packt is a modern, yet unique publishing company, which focuses on producing quality, cutting-edge books for communities of developers, administrators, and newbies alike. For more information, please visit our website: www.packtpub.com.

# About Packt Open Source

In 2010, Packt launched two new brands, Packt Open Source and Packt Enterprise, in order to continue its focus on specialization. This book is part of the Packt Open Source brand, home to books published on software built around Open Source licenses, and offering information to anybody from advanced developers to budding web designers. The Open Source brand also runs Packt's Open Source Royalty Scheme, by which Packt gives a royalty to each Open Source project about whose software a book is sold.

# Writing for Packt

We welcome all inquiries from people who are interested in authoring. Book proposals should be sent to author@packtpub.com. If your book idea is still at an early stage and you would like to discuss it first before writing a formal book proposal, contact us; one of our commissioning editors will get in touch with you.

We're not just looking for published authors; if you have strong technical skills but no writing experience, our experienced editors can help you develop a writing career, or simply get some additional reward for your expertise.

## Learning Python Data Visualization

ISBN: 978-1-78355-333-4        Paperback: 212 pages

Master how to build dynamic HTML5-ready SVG charts using Python and the pygal library

1. A practical guide that helps you break into the world of data visualization with Python.

2. Understand the fundamentals of building charts in Python.

3. Packed with easy-to-understand tutorials for developers who are new to Python or charting in Python.

## Learning scikit-learn: Machine Learning in Python

ISBN: 978-1-78328-193-0        Paperback: 118 pages

Experience the benefits of machine learning techniques by applying them to real-world problems using Python and the open source scikit-learn library

1. Use Python and scikit-learn to create intelligent applications.

2. Apply regression techniques to predict future behavior and learn to cluster items in groups by their similarities.

3. Make use of classification techniques to perform image recognition and document classification.

Please check **www.PacktPub.com** for information on our titles

## IPython Interactive Computing and Visualization Cookbook

ISBN: 978-1-78328-481-8　　　Paperback: 512 pages

Over 100 hands-on recipes to sharpen your skills in high-performance numerical computing and data science with Python

1. Leverage the new features of the IPython Notebook for interactive web-based Big Data analysis and visualization.

2. Become an expert in high-performance computing and visualization for data analysis and scientific modeling.

3. A comprehensive coverage of scientific computing through many hands-on, example-driven recipes with detailed, step-by-step explanations.

## Building Machine Learning Systems with Python

ISBN: 978-1-78216-140-0　　　Paperback: 290 pages

Master the art of machine learning with Python and build effective machine learning systems with this intensive hands-on guide

1. Helps you master machine learning using a broad set of Python libraries and start building your own Python-based ML systems.

2. Covers classification, regression, feature engineering, and much more guided by practical examples.

3. A scenario-based tutorial to get into the right mind-set of a machine learner (data exploration) and successfully implement this in your new or existing projects.

Please check **www.PacktPub.com** for information on our titles

CPSIA information can be obtained
at www.ICGtesting.com
Printed in the USA
LVOW04s1701301117
558160LV00005B/383/P